THE
WINE
FLAVOUR
GUIDE

SAM
CAPORN

For Mum, My Guiding Star

THE
WINE
FLAVOUR
GUIDE

HOW TO PICK THE BEST WINE FOR EVERY OCCASION

SAM
CAPORN

 SQUARE PEG

1 3 5 7 9 10 8 6 4 2

Square Peg, an imprint of Vintage, is part of the Penguin Random House group of companies whose addresses can be found at global.penguinrandomhouse.com

First published by Square Peg in 2024

Book design by Lucy Sykes-Thompson of Studio Polka

penguin.co.uk/vintage

Printed and bound by Papercraft, Malaysia

The authorised representative in the EEA is Penguin Random House Ireland, Morrison Chambers, 32 Nassau Street, Dublin D02 YH68

A CIP catalogue record for this book is available from the British Library

ISBN 9781529913460

Penguin Random House is committed to a sustainable future for our business, our readers and our planet. This book is made from Forest Stewardship Council® certified paper.

At Christmas I no more desire a rose
Than wish a snow in May's new-fangled mirth;
But like of each thing that in season grows.

WILLIAM SHAKESPEARE,
LOVE'S LABOUR'S LOST,
1.1.103–105

CONTENTS

WELCOME

'The Mistress of Wine': My Background	10
Picking the Best Wines for Every Occasion	12
The Wine Flavour Tree	14
How to Use This Book	16

Part 1 – Wine 101: Your Guide to All Things Wine

AN INTRODUCTION TO WINE

Anatomy of a Wine	20
The Wine Flavour Tree: Your Ultimate Grape Guide	24
Terroir in a Nutshell	34
In the Vineyard: Organic, Biodynamic & Sustainable Viticulture	36
Wine Science: How Different Wines are Made	39

HOW TO FIND THE BEST BOTTLE FOR YOU, ON ANY BUDGET

How to Understand a Wine Label: Varietal vs Regional Labelling	62
Decoding Your Wine Bottle	74
Cost and Quality	76
Common Wine Faults	78
Storing and Serving Wine	80
Different Bottle Sizes	86

EVERYTHING YOU NEED TO KNOW ABOUT WINE TASTING

Introduction	52
How to 'Taste' Wine for Ultimate Enjoyment	54

FOOD AND WINE PAIRING 101

Introduction	87
Final Thoughts on Food and Wine: Matching the Seasons	90

Part 2 – A Wine for Every Season and Occasion

SPRING

What's Happening in the Vineyard?	100
Spring Wine Styles: Whites	101
Spring Wine Styles: Reds	109
Spring Food and Wine Matching	118
Spring Recipes	121
Other Spring Wine Styles: Sparkling Wines	126

SUMMER

What's Happening in the Vineyard?	138
Summer Wine Styles: Whites	139
Summer Wine Styles: Reds	155
Summer Food and Wine Matching	162
Summer Recipes	165
Other Summer Wine Styles: Rosé Wines	172

AUTUMN

What's Happening in the Vineyard?	178
Autumn Wine Styles: Whites	179
Autumn Wine Styles: Reds	189
Autumn Food and Wine Matching	198
Autumn Recipes	201
Other Autumn Wine Styles: Orange Wines	208

WINTER

What's Happening in the Vineyard?	216
Winter Wine Styles: Whites	217
Winter Wine Styles: Reds	225
Winter Food and Wine Matching	242
Winter Recipes	245
Other Winter Wine Styles: Fortified and Sweet Wines	254

PAIRING WINE WITH EVERY FOOD

Poultry	268
Fish & Seafood	270
Red Meat, Pork & Game	272
Vegetables	274
Cheese & Dairy	276
Puddings & Desserts	278

YOUR WINE DICTIONARY

The Structure of Wine	282
Common Wine Faults	284
Other Lingo	285
Wine Tasting Templates	290
Index	294
Acknowledgements	302
About the Author	304

WELCOME

What wines do you inherently tend to prefer? Do you like an exuberant, effervescent fizz that sparkles and dances across your tongue? Or a rich, tannic red that lingers in your mouth with notes of spicy oak? Perhaps a vivid, eclectic, textured, orange wine that bursts with flavours of dried fruits and apricots, or a delicate dry white?

Whatever your favourite style of wine, *The Wine Flavour Guide* will help you to better understand why you like the wines that you do, by detailing and describing the different flavours and structures inherent in a wide range of popular grape varieties. These are then put into ten 'flavour families', grouped together according to a shared flavour profile and displayed on the Wine Flavour Tree, an infographic that I created to make understanding your wine that bit easier. It will also help with wider experimentation – taking you outside your comfort zone, by identifying and introducing you to new varieties that you are likely to appreciate.

When it comes to wine, personal preference is fundamental to enjoyment, appreciation and understanding – it really is a matter of taste. The taste buds in your mouth – estimated to number between 2,000 and 10,000, which are replaced on average every two weeks – coupled with specific inbuilt responses to things like bitterness (people differ genetically in their sensitivity to certain chemical compounds, along with not being able to taste or identify certain smells or tastes) are likely to result in you having favourite grape varieties and preferred wine styles. Individuals with more taste buds are known as 'supertasters', which actually means that they are more sensitive, rather than being better at tasting, and then there are 'average' tasters and 'non-tasters', the latter those who have fewer taste buds than the norm.

Unsurprisingly, this tasting ability affects your appreciation of everything you put in your mouth, not just wine, and in the same way that supertasters might not like the bitterness of chicory or watercress or the tartness of grapefruit, such preferences will be carried across to wine too. It stands to reason that people who have more taste buds are likely to lean towards wines that are more subtle and understated. Meanwhile, non-tasters might typically order the strongest, spiciest curries and intense, inky, full-bodied tannic wines with plenty of structure and flavour that pack a bit of a punch; while average tasters can happily play across a fairly wide flavour and structure spectrum.

What about you – do you recognise yourself as falling into one of these categories of tasters? Perhaps you were deemed a picky or sensitive eater, or conversely, have you always enjoyed a wide range of different flavours, textures and tastes? For me – luckily – I think I'm largely average but inch towards super (I suspect I have a just above normal number of taste buds), as I enjoy a wide range of different foods and wine but am not a fan of certain styles – usually those with elevated acidity or bitter, drying tannins. For my job, being a really sensitive taster would actually be a disadvantage, as I would dislike too many wines.

I once sat next to someone at a dinner who was mortified to admit that she only liked, and consequently only drank, Pinot Grigio. While it might be a bit unusual to stick to just one grape variety for all occasions and meals, it's certainly not unusual to prefer a handful of different types of wine to others – and good for her for knowing what she liked and not succumbing to peer pressure. Indeed, you too may already know what kind of wines you prefer, but even if you don't – especially if you don't – this book is for you.

'The Mistress of Wine': My Background

Rest assured that you are in safe hands as you join me on this journey of wine discovery! I have been in the wine trade for almost three decades – after university, I wanted to travel and write, and as I had run the university's wine society with a couple of friends, my mum wisely suggested I unite all three elements and go into the industry. Since that time I have gone from knowing pretty much nothing about wine to becoming a bonefide wine expert: a Master of Wine (MW). A lot of people think that means I'm a sommelier but the two things are very different. Sommeliers largely work in restaurants, predominantly in fine-dining establishments, advising guests on the wine list and matching wines to food. A Master of Wine can work anywhere, but in order to become one, eight rigorous exams need to be passed, three practical and five theory.

The practical exams each consist of blind-tasting twelve different wines – essentially having to identify what's in the glass by looking at, smelling and tasting the wine and then answering specific questions on it, usually on grape variety or varieties, where it is from, quality, how it was made and possibly vintage. There is a white wine exam, a red wine exam and a miscellaneous exam (which when I sat showed three rosé wines for the first time but could also show sparkling or sweet wines). The five theory papers test your knowledge of viticulture (in the vineyard), vinification (in the winery), the handling of wine, the business of wine and contemporary issues. If you're successful in the theory papers you're permitted to start on a 10,000-word research paper; only when this has been completed and passed are you entitled to add the prestigious 'MW' to your name.

More people have been into space than are Masters of Wine: there are currently just over 400 Masters of Wine in the world, of which only about 150 are women. I became a Master of Wine in 2011 and was also awarded the Madame Bollinger Medal for Excellence in Tasting and for Outstanding Achievement in the Practical Examinations, a much coveted prize that is awarded to the individual who performed the best among their peers in the blind tasting or practical exams. I am one of only sixteen women globally to have ever been awarded this medal.

Today I'm a freelance wine consultant, and among other things I work with a major UK discounter, judge wines as a co-chair at the International Wine Competition and host corporate wine tastings. I chose to call myself the 'Mistress of Wine' both as a play on words and to reflect my passion as an educator.

Unsurprisingly, people are often curious to know what wines I enjoy, and I'm frequently asked whether I have a favourite wine. While I don't have a single most-loved bottle or producer, I do absolutely have preferred grape varieties and favourite geographical regions. My desert island wine would indisputably be a bottle of rather pricey, bottle-aged vintage champagne (ideally paid for by someone else), while for day-to-day drinking my whites tend to be made from Chardonnay (white burgundy from France or cool-climate southern hemisphere bottles from South Africa or Australia). When it comes to reds, I love Spanish Rioja, French Syrah (especially from the Northern Rhône) and warm-climate Cabernet Sauvignon (hello, California and South Australia).

All of these are united by being medium- to full-bodied and flavourful without being wildly aromatic. They also have moderate acidity and no harsh edges or tight tannins (that drying sensation around the sides or your mouth that you get from some red wines and also tea), and are frequently fermented and/or matured in oak, which brings a sprinkling of spice to the wines. They are 'cosy' wines, providing pleasure and the vinous equivalent of a warm jumper and slippers. But despite these innate preferences, I don't actually wish to drink my favourite wines *all* the time – from heady hot summer days through to freezing-cold, frosty nights. Instead, I prefer something different depending on the weather, the situation and the occasion, and I'd say that's true for most of us.

Picking the Best Wines for Every Occasion

Each season brings with it special occasions – times for celebration or reflection – and provides an abundance of different fresh foods. As the weather changes, and with it our mood, so too does what we want to eat and drink. Warmer weather generally makes people crave lighter food with a higher water content, from spring greens, spinach, herbs and asparagus which mirror the fecund rebirth and new green shoots of the season to the cornucopia of fruits, vegetables and salads that mark the arrival of summer. All can be used to create dishes that are refreshing and simple to make; who wants to be stuck in a hot kitchen making fiddly food on a gorgeous summer's day?

Conversely, in colder months food is richer, fuller and a touch stodgier, and consequently the flavour and structure of the wines we choose need to intensify, to prevent them being overwhelmed by more robust dishes. Autumn's amber bounty, harvested and gathered at the same time as the ripened grapes, includes butternut squash, pumpkins and parsnips, while winter is synonymous with sprouts – the most loved or loathed of all vegetables – as well as cabbage, kale and leeks. Indeed, as autumn gives way to winter's short days and long nights, carbs become king, along with a desire for comfort foods, as our bodies want to hibernate and store reserves – and the wines we drink need to be able to hold their own. Ultimately, different types of wine match better with different foods. Perky, zesty whites marry well with spring's herbs, and of course summer's favourite, dry rosé – the archetypal, subtly flavoured, refreshing wine – goes best with the lighter, fresher dishes of summer. Richer whites or orange wines are ideal in the autumn – they pair brilliantly with root vegetables or risotto – and winter generally means full-bodied reds. The same principle also applies when eating a dish in the 'wrong' season; spring lamb still marries brilliantly with spring reds, even if eaten in the autumn.

Threaded through the seasons are cultural and religious events firmly embedded in and associated with that time of the year. Spring welcomes the cherry blossoms in Japan, Mother's Day, Easter and Passover. Summer is largely a celebration in its own right, from BBQs and festivals (music, food and literary) to packed beaches full of people basking in the serotonin-boosting effect of the sun's rays, the season is giddy and full of fun. Autumn celebrates beautiful Diwali, Halloween, the Day of the Dead, Guy Fawkes and Thanksgiving. Winter has an abundance of festivals that meet the human need for comfort and cheering up to counteract the dark days and long nights, such as Hanukkah, Christmas, New Year or Hogmanay, Burns Night and Chinese New Year.

So remember, when you are celebrating throughout the year, look to the season to help you select that superlative bottle of wine with which to enjoy your food, but also, to raise a glass with.

The Wine Flavour Tree

The Wine Flavour Guide is very much a celebration of the changing seasons and the special moments and cultural occasions that fall within them, influencing what we want to eat and drink, acting as signposts, guiding and leading us through the year, giving it shape and form. It looks at how the flavour and structure of grape varieties pair particularly well with specific seasons and their produce, underpinning – as so many wine lovers will recognise – why drinking patterns are usually seasonal, evolving as the year progresses. The second part of this book is therefore organised by season. The first part is my guide to all things wine and contains a unique infographic – my Wine Flavour Tree.

I designed the Wine Flavour Tree to help wine lovers navigate the world of wine flavour. As a wine expert you are taught to recognise aromas, flavours and structure in order to assess identity and quality, but for imbibers rather than professionals, it's all too easy to smell or 'nose' a glass and simply smell 'just wine'. Because wine is made from different grape varieties, it smells and tastes of different things. The aromas and flavours that are inherent in wine are predominantly fruit and flower based. The Wine Flavour Tree provides clear signposts to help you recognise these smells and tastes, so as to better find your favourites.

How to read the wine flavour tree

The infographic is shaped like a tree and has a total of ten branches (five on each side) with four flavour icons on each branch, grouped together according to a commonality of flavour. Each branch is given a name – such as Stone Fruits – and these names can be found under the Tree, accompanied by the names of four grape varieties that these flavours are

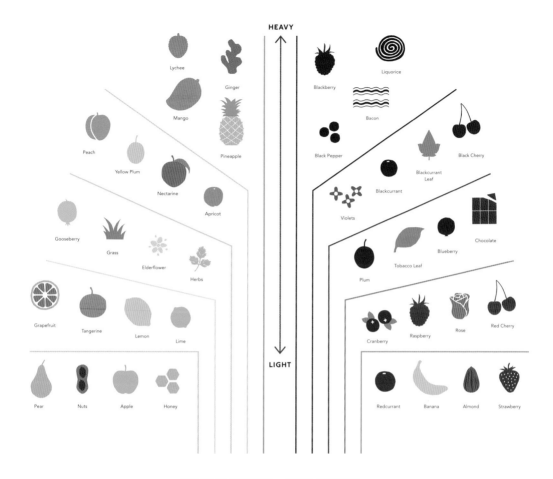

HEAVY

Lychee
Ginger
Mango
Pineapple
Peach
Yellow Plum
Nectarine
Apricot
Gooseberry
Grass
Elderflower
Herbs
Grapefruit
Tangerine
Lemon
Lime
Pear
Nuts
Apple
Honey

Blackberry
Liquorice
Bacon
Black Pepper
Blackcurrant Leaf
Black Cherry
Blackcurrant
Violets
Chocolate
Tobacco Leaf
Blueberry
Plum
Cranberry
Raspberry
Rose
Red Cherry
Redcurrant
Banana
Almond
Strawberry

LIGHT

WHITE WINES

ORCHARD FRUITS
Pinot Grigio, unoaked Chardonnay, Garganega, Chenin Blanc

CITRUS FRUITS
Grüner Veltliner, Falanghina, Sémillon, dry Riesling

GREEN FRUITS & GRASS
Sauvignon Blanc, Verdejo, Bacchus, Vermentino

STONE FRUITS
Chardonnay, Fiano, Viognier, Albariño

EXOTIC FRUITS & SPICE
Gewürztraminer, Torrontés, Muscat, off-dry Riesling

RED WINES

SOFT & JUICY
Cinsault, Gamay, Dolcetto, Tarrango

RED FRUITS & ROSES
Pinot Noir, Grenache, Nebbiolo, Sangiovese

BERRIES & CHOCOLATE
Merlot, Tempranillo, Barbera, Nero d'Avola

CURRANTS & HERBS
Cabernet Sauvignon, Touriga Nacional, Carménère, Negroamaro

BLACKBERRIES & SPICE
Malbec, Zinfandel, Shiraz, Syrah, Pinotage

frequently found in. So, not only can the Tree help you to recognise the aromas and flavours present in a wine, it can also aid with experimentation by suggesting other grape varieties with a similar flavour profile.

In total forty flavours are depicted, with the left-hand side showing those present in white wines and the right-hand side those occurring in reds. The flavours and structure of wines made from these varieties increase as you travel up the Tree, with the lower branches showing flavours that are typically found in lighter-bodied, more subtle and restrained wines, while those at the top of the Tree indicate flavours present in full-throttled, more robust styles. Crucially, the four different – but united – flavours on each branch marry with the flavours of the fresh produce found in one of the four seasons, making wines with these flavours ideal for drinking within them. As such, each branch of the Tree is allocated a specific season that it suits the most.

How to Use This Book

Before we dive into the Wine Flavour Tree in full, we'll start with a really useful Wine 101 looking at what wine actually *is*, how it is made and why it tastes the way it does, as well as providing essential wine know-how while also answering a number of questions along the way:

1. What are the 'legs' of a wine and does having them mean that the wine is better? (p. 21)
2. What is tannin? (pp. 22–3)
3. What is terroir? (p. 34)
4. What makes a wine biodynamic? (p. 37)
5. Why is some wine white but some red (or even orange or pink)? (pp. 42–9)
6. What is 'skin contact'? (pp. 45–6)
7. What does it mean if a wine is 'corked'? (pp. 58–9)
8. What is regional labelling? (pp. 62–4)
9. What does 'vintage' mean? (p. 64)

10. How do you 'read' a wine label? (pp. 66–7)
11. What are the key factors that inform wine quality? (pp. 76–7)
12. What bearing do prices have on wines? (pp. 76–7)
13. Do you have to decant wines? (p. 83)
14. How long can you leave wine once open? (pp. 84–5)
15. How do I match wine with food? (pp. 87–9)

Some common wine myths will also be debunked, including the one
I probably get asked about the most – does putting a spoon in your bottle
of fizz keep it sparkling?! Part 1 concludes with some general advice about
food and wine pairing in advance of the seasonal sections of Part 2.

This book is intended as your handbook to enjoying wine. It can be
read cover to cover or dipped into; you may wish to head straight to the
current season for inspiration for a bottle of wine for dinner with a partner
or friends, or be looking for a simple recipe with which to pair it. You might
want a quick refresher on wine terminology or how to understand wine
labels while shopping for wine, whether that be online, in the supermarket
or visiting your local independent merchant. Or perhaps you'll use the Wine
Flavour Tree to identify the flavour in your glass or find something else
you think you'd love. However this book is approached, by using it as your
guide it will give you the confidence to choose the best wine for each and
every occasion, helping you to drink that ideal bottle of wine all year long.

Let's get started!

Sam Caporn MW
The Mistress of Wine

Wine 101: Your Guide to All Things Wine

PART 1

AN INTRODUCTION TO WINE

Anatomy of a Wine

What *is* wine? Wine is an alcoholic beverage made when yeasts convert the sugars found in grapes (the berries of the grape vine) into alcohol through fermentation. Surprisingly, the major component of wine is actually water, which makes up about 85 per cent of the liquid in each bottle of wine. The balance is comprised of alcohol, glycerol, residual sugar, acidity and tiny but crucial amounts of flavour compounds and phenolics – colour and tannins. Before we delve any further into the winemaking process (see p. 39), let's discuss some of these terms.

Grapes

One of the many wonderful things about wine is how versatile and varied it can be – taste, style, colour and price can differ hugely even though all wines start life as the same thing: a bunch of grapes. Wine vines – or *Vitis vinifera*, of which there are thousands of different varities such as Chardonnay, Pinot Noir, Sauvignon Blanc and Merlot – are grown all over the world. They are essentially an agricultural product and therefore are very much subject to the vagaries of the weather and the broader climate of the region where the vineyard is situated. Grapes grown in warmer regions closer to the equator benefit from more sun, and I like to think of them as sunbathing – sitting on the vine, enjoying the sunshine and getting fat and juicy. They ripen well and have more sugar and less acidity. On the other hand, grapes grown in cooler climates tend to be the opposite and so have less sugar, higher acidity and are typically lighter: leaner and more elegant. Irrespective of where they are grown, the colourless flesh of the grapes is very important, for not only does it provide the all-important sugars, it also contains water and the grape's acidity.

DID YOU KNOW? The quality of the final wine is fundamentally determined by the quality of the grapes grown in the vineyard; it is hard to make bad wine out of good grapes!

Alcohol

Very simplistically, during the winemaking process the sugar in grapes is fermented via the action of yeasts and turned into alcohol (ethanol). The higher the sugar levels in the grapes, the higher the alcohol in the wine. Wines made from grapes high in sugar tend to be medium- or full-bodied, with more power, structure and 'oomph'. The opposite is true for wines made with grapes that have less sugar – they are likely to be lighter in body and fresher. Alcohol also provides viscosity and texture; the 'legs' or 'tears' that can be seen on the side of a wine glass only indicate alcoholic strength (or sweetness), not quality. It is also worth remembering that it's the excessive consumption of alcohol that contributes to a hangover, not the price or quality of a wine, nor whether it is organic or contains sulphites. (Turn to p. 50 for more on this.)

Residual sugar

The term residual sugar refers predominantly to the sugars remaining in a wine after the fermentation has finished. Sometimes the winemaker will intervene to stop the fermentation in order to achieve a certain style of wine. This happens in the production of port, for example, where the fermentation is arrested by the addition of a neutral grape spirit. This not only means the wine remains sweet, but also boosts its alcohol content – which 'fortifies' it. Some commercial wines have their sweetness levels boosted post-fermentation through the addition of grape concentrate, which can make them taste 'softer' and gives a slight tutti frutti character to the wine.

Glycerol

Glycerol is a by-product of fermentation and performs a similar role to both alcohol and residual sugar insofar as it contributes to the smoothness and 'mouthfeel' of a wine.

Acidity

The main acids found in wine are tartaric, malic and citric and winemakers measure acidity by using the pH scale. When drinking wine, acidity can be detected at the sides of the tongue and it can also make your mouth water.

Tannins

Aside from the grape flesh or pulp the skins of grapes also play an extremely important role in determining the characteristics or 'personality' of a wine. The skins not only contain the flavour compounds (which play a major role in how a wine tastes) but also the colour – anthocyanins – and tannins. Tannins are present in the grape seeds and stalks too, and are also added to the wine in oak fermentation and maturation. They are felt predominantly around the sides of the mouth as a slightly drying sensation, similar to when drinking tea. They are also essential to the ageing of red wines, as it is when the tannins polymerise that wine softens and mellows. Polymerisation is when the tannin molecules bind together and form long chains which become too heavy to remain suspended in the wine, so they break down leaving sediment – which you can sometimes see at the bottom of your glass. This is why many older wines need decanting.

Balance and wine quality

For a wine to be good or even great, the main components that make up its anatomy – the acidity, sweetness, alcohol, tannins and fruit concentration – all need to be in **balance**; one part cannot overwhelm the others. Indeed, balance is one of the most important (but possibly underrated) elements of wine. Another indicator of quality is **length**: how long can you can taste it for after swallowing? You want to be able to taste it for a while – the longer the better. Then there's **intensity** – how concentrated is the wine, especially in the middle of the mouth? You don't want the wine to be dilute or hollow in the mid-palate – this is known as a doughnut wine. And finally, **complexity** – how layered, nuanced and interesting is it? Can you taste multiple different flavours?

> **TIP** To assess the quality of a wine when tasting it, think BLIC – Balance, Length, Intensity, Complexity.

The Wine Flavour Tree:
Your Ultimate Grape Guide

When it comes to choosing wine, the only thing that really matters is getting to know the styles and flavours that you like and why. If you're not sure what they are yet, start off by asking yourself some fairly broad questions – you'll be able to overlay these against the Tree later on:

- Do I like acidity in my white wines? Some are crisper and more citrussy than others.
- Do I generally prefer easy-drinking wines with more delicate flavours?
- Do I like my red wines to be smooth or a bit richer and more full-bodied? And in terms of flavour, do I tend to prefer red, blue, purple or black fruits?
- And what about riper, softer and even sweeter whites?

If I had to pick just one thing that contributes most significantly to the flavour of a wine, then it would have to be the grape variety or blend of varieties that make up that individual wine. Without a doubt, there are other really important factors to consider too, such as the soil, the climate and whether the wine has been fermented and/or matured in oak, but the grape variety is responsible for the innate personality of a wine. Getting to know these varieties will help you to identify wines that suit your palate, the season and occasion.

Grape varieties

There are over 10,000 different varieties that belong to the common grape vine species although fortunately, when it comes to trying to identify your favourites, wine is only made from a tiny fraction of them! Think of the different grape varieties as being like apples: just as you have many types of apples – Pink Lady, Cox, Braeburn, Gala, Golden Delicious, Granny Smith – which are all subtly different, it is the same with grapes. You have the generic grape vine but then you also have different varieties such as Chenin Blanc, Sauvignon Blanc, Pinot Grigio, Cabernet Sauvignon, Pinotage, Gamay etc., and each one smells and tastes slightly different.

Predominantly, but not exclusively, grape varieties contribute aromas and flavours reminiscent of a range of fruits, as well as flowers and herbs. Aroma and flavour compounds are not only present in the skins and juice of the grape but are also produced during the winemaking process. Learning which grape varieties are likely to smell and taste of which fruits makes identifying those flavours far easier, and can therefore enhance wine appreciation.

As well as providing different aromas and flavours, the grape varieties are also responsible, in conjunction with where they are grown, for the weight and body of a wine, as well as its colour. Thin-skinned grapes tend to produce lighter coloured wines and if they have big berries too – such as Pinot Noir – then the wines will also be lighter in weight and structure. This is because of the **skin-to-pulp ratio**: large, thin-skinned grapes make softer wines because the colour, flavour and tannins found in the skins are essentially diluted by the grape's pulp. Smaller berries with thicker skins, however, make wines that are deeper in colour, more tannic and with a richer fruit profile such as Caberent Sauvignon and Syrah.

DID YOU KNOW? Wine can either be made from a single grape variety or from a blend of different ones. Châteauneuf-du-Pape in France is famously allowed to include up to thirteen different varieties. A wine is not necessarily better or worse if it is a blend, it is just different.

Where does the flavour in wine actually come from?

The flavour of a wine comes from both the grapes themselves and the winemaking process. The main products of fermentation are alcohol and carbon dioxide, but alongside these, hundreds of chemical compounds called **esters** are also created, and some of these are **volatile**, meaning you can smell them. It is these volatile esters which essentially make up a wine's flavour, as flavour is created from aroma (smell) coupled with taste.

Aroma + Taste = Flavour

There are hundreds of different aromas in wine and, if you are new to trying to identify them, even recognising a few key aromas can pose a challenge. For many people they simply 'smell wine', at least at first. While some flavours that tasters say they can detect in wine are fanciful at best, the majority are absolutely present in your glass. Here are some examples of the chemical names of various flavour compounds that are found in wine and are shown on the Wine Flavour Tree:

FLAVOUR NOTE	CHEMICAL COMPOUND
ALMOND	Benzaldehyde
APPLE	Butyl acetate
BLACKCURRANT	4MMP (4-mercapto-4-methylpentan-2-one)
BLACK PEPPER	Rotundone
ELDERFLOWER	Hotrienol
GOOSEBERRY	3MHA (3-mercaptohexyl acetate)
HERBS	Methoxypyrazine
LEMON	Citral + limonene
ROSE	Damascenone + geraniol
TANGERINE	Octyl acetate
VIOLETS	Linalool + beta ionone
GRAPEFRUIT	3MHA (3-mer-captohexan-1-ol)

How does the Wine Flavour Tree work?

You can learn to recognise aromas in wines by acquainting yourself with the most popular grape varieties and their flavours. And this is what the Wine Flavour Tree does: the Tree shows forty distinct flavours – from apricot, to gooseberry, blackcurrant and even bacon – that can be detected in different wines from around the world. Divided into two parts, the left-hand side depicts twenty flavours found in wines made from **white varietals** (such as Bacchus and Fiano), and the right-hand side shows twenty flavours typically found in those made from specific **red varietals** (think Malbec and Grenache).

The Tree has five branches on each side and on each of these are four flavour icons which have been grouped together because of a commonality of flavour. Each branch has a name to reflect this shared flavour profile, such as Stone Fruits – peach, yellow plum, nectarine and apricot – or Citrus Fruits – grapefruit, tangerine, lemon and lime – and is a different colour. Underneath the name of each branch opposite are four grape varieties that typically, although not exclusively, display the flavours depicted by the icons on the branch when made into wine. For example, the flavours found on the Citrus Fruits branch are present in Grüner Veltliner, Falanghina, Sémillon and dry Riesling.

The intensity of the flavours increases the further up the Tree you go, getting stronger and more distinctive, while the structure of the wines becomes heavier and richer too. So full-bodied reds and their flavours are found on the top-right branch of the Tree, while lighter wines with subtler flavours such as pear and apples or strawberry and redcurrant belong to the bottom branches on both sides.

Each branch of the Wine Flavour Tree is also suited to a specific season of the year due to the flavours and structure of the varieties associated with it. The flavours work with the season's fresh produce, and the weight of the wines pair well with the food generally eaten at that time of year. The branches of the Wine Flavour Tree with their ideal seasons are shown opposite:

WHITE WINE BRANCHES

Orchard Fruits (pear, nuts, apple, honey);
Pinot Grigio, unoaked Chardonnay, Garganega, Chenin Blanc – **SUMMER**

Citrus Fruits (grapefruit, tangerine, lemon, lime);
Grüner Veltliner, Falanghina, Sémillon, dry Riesling – **SUMMER**

Green Fruits & Grass (gooseberry, grass, elderflower, herbs)
Sauvignon Blanc, Verdejo, Bacchus, Vermentino – **SPRING**

Stone Fruits (peach, yellow plum, nectarine, apricot);
Chardonnay, Fiano, Viognier, Albariño – **AUTUMN**

Exotic Fruits & Spice (lychee, ginger, mango, pineapple);
Gewürztraminer, Torrontés, Muscat, off-dry Riesling – **WINTER**

RED WINE BRANCHES

Soft & Juicy (redcurrant, banana, almond, strawberry);
Cinsault, Gamay, Dolcetto, Tarrango – **SUMMER**

Red Fruits & Roses (cranberry, raspberry, rose, red cherry);
Pinot Noir, Grenache, Nebbiolo, Sangiovese – **WINTER**

Berries & Chocolate (plum, tobacco leaf, blueberry, chocolate);
Merlot, Tempranillo, Barbera, Nero D'Avola – **AUTUMN**

Currants & Herbs (violets, blackcurrant, blackcurrant leaf, black cherry);
Cabernet Sauvignon, Touriga Nacional, Carménère, Negroamaro – **SPRING**

Blackberries & Spice (black pepper, bacon, blackberry, liquorice);
Malbec, Zinfandel, Shiraz/Syrah, Pinotage – **WINTER**

THE WINE FLAVOUR TREE

Lychee

Ginger

Mango

Pineapple

Peach

Yellow Plum

Nectarine

Apricot

Gooseberry

Grass

Elderflower

Herbs

Grapefruit

Tangerine

Lemon

Lime

Pear

Nuts

Apple

Honey

HEAVY

Blackberry

Liquorice

Bacon

Black Pepper

Black Cherry

Blackcurrant
Leaf

Blackcurrant

Violets

Chocolate

Blueberry

Tobacco Leaf

Plum

Cranberry

Raspberry

Rose

Red Cherry

Redcurrant

Banana

Almond

Strawberry

LIGHT

IDENTIFYING YOUR FAVOURITE WINES

By now you will hopefully have a clearer idea of the flavours you prefer, the grape varieties that deliver those flavours and the best time of year to drink the wines you love. The Tree also assists with experimentation, as the grape varieties are grouped together according to what they taste like.

So if you enjoy a Sauvignon Blanc, for example, locate it on the **Green Fruits & Grass** branch and see what other varieties are on there too, as they will have flavours in common. This might then encourage you to try an elderflower and herb-scented English Bacchus, potentially leading to the discovery of a new favourite.

Now, let's return to the questions I asked at the beginning of this section – and use the Wine Flavour Tree to answer them.

Q: Do I like acidity in my white wines? Some are crisper and more citrussy than others.

A: If you like higher-acidity wines, then look at the lower to middle branches of the Tree such as **Citrus Fruits** and **Green Fruits & Grass** as you will appreciate the tangy, zesty and herbal flavours as well as the fresher, crisper character of the wines.

Q: Do I generally prefer easy-drinking wines with more delicate flavours?

A: If this is the case, stick to the bottom branches of the Tree on both sides – **Orchard Fruits** and **Soft & Juicy** – as with their subtle aromas and unchallenging structures these wines will be great for you.

Q: Do I like my red wines to be smooth or a bit richer and more full-bodied? And in terms of flavour, do I tend to prefer red, blue, purple or black fruits?

A: If you have a preference for smooth reds, look to the middle of the Tree and the **Berries & Chocolate** branch in particular, where the wines are medium-bodied and round. For richer, more full-bodied reds, the **Currants & Herbs** and **Blackberries & Spice** branches are for you. For red fruits look to the **Red Fruits & Roses** branch; for blue and purple fruit choose **Berries & Chocolate** and for black fruits both the **Currants & Herbs** and **Blackberries & Spice** branches deliver rich, velvety fruit and warmer, bigger styles.

Q: And what about riper, softer and even sweeter whites?

A: For riper whites with peachy, stone fruit flavours that are medium- to full-bodied then the **Stone Fruits** branch is both succulent and juicy, whereas **Exotic Fruits & Spice** will cater for all your off-dry needs.

Terroir in a Nutshell

Although the grape variety is what predominantly affects how a wine tastes, where in the world those grapes are grown is also important to the taste of the resultant wine. For instance, a Chardonnay from Chablis will taste quite different to one from California.

The French term terroir essentially means a 'sense of place' and encompasses the natural elements of the vineyard site where the grapes are grown, which contribute significantly to the grapes' flavour. One of the main factors of terroir that influences these subtle variations in taste is the climate, including both the wider conditions in the region and the more specific microclimate.

Another huge part of terroir is the soil: from slate, to marl, to clay, to chalk and gravel. Different grape varieties have affinities with different soils, and this largely dictates where they are grown. Riesling likes slate, Chardonnay chalk and Cabernet Sauvignon gravel, for example.

The topography of the vineyard, in particular its aspect – the direction in which any slope faces – is the final main element that comprises terroir. In cooler wine-producing regions in the northern hemisphere, it is the vaunted south-facing slopes that are favoured, as they help the grapes to ripen. The opposite is true in the southern hemisphere, where a more northerly aspect is an advantage.

Terroir = Climate + Soil + Aspect

Yield

Whilst the climate, soil and aspect make up a vineyard's terroir, something else that is really useful to understand is yield. Yield is simply the volume of grapes harvested within a specific area and is commonly measured in hectolitres or tonnes per hectare. As a rule of thumb, the higher the yield (that is, the greater the quantity) the lower the quality, and vice versa. There will be years when both quality and quantity can be achieved, but typically you have to sacrifice one for the other.

Lower yield (quantity of fruit) =

higher quality of wine

DID YOU KNOW? Poor soils can actually be beneficial to vine growing as they force the vine's roots to go deep into the soil to reach those all-important nutrients.

In the Vineyard: Organic, Biodynamic & Sustainable Viticulture

Organic practices

When it comes to viticulture – the growing and harvesting of grapes – there are a number of different diseases and pests that can wreak havoc. Consequently fungicides and pesticides are commonly used in conventional vineyards to either prevent or treat problems.

Some growers however are concerned about the use of fungicides, pesticides and fertilisers in agriculture and have adopted alternative strategies.

Organic wine is wine that is made from organically grown grapes, which means that no synthetic chemicals are used to grow the fruit, and composts are used for soil health instead of fertilisers. In most of the world, the term 'organic wine' allows a certain amount of sulphites to be added to the finished wine. However, in the United States and Canada, the organic wine label also means that it has no added sulphur. If sulphur has been added, the term 'made with organic grapes' has to be employed instead.

Biodynamic practices

Another approach is 'biodynamic agriculture'. Based on the theories of the Austrian occultist and social reformer Rudolf Steiner, biodynamic agriculture takes organic grape growing one step further. Practitioners believe that the vineyard or farm is a living and self-sustaining entity, and place huge emphasis on soil health. Whilst both organic and biodynamic farming eschew the use of synthetic chemicals, biodynamic farming relies on a number of special, natural preparations, which are used either as a compost or a spray. The sprays have to be dynamised (vigorously stirred in different directions to harness energy) before they are ready for application, whilst the composts do not. The preparations are used according to the different phases of the moon to ensure optimal grape and vineyard health.

The position of the moon is also believed to affect the actual drinking and appreciation of wine. The moon's pull over water is well documented – from the tides of the sea to human behaviour – and wine is made up of 85 per cent water. Look for the official Demeter or Biodyvin labels on wine bottles to ensure biodynamic certification.

Regenerative viticulture, which may be conventional, organic or biodynamic, also looks to improve soil health and biodiversity but without the 'mysticism' associated with biodynamics. *Lutte raisonée* simply sees growers trying to be more sustainable by aiming to use fewer chemicals in the vineyards.

Neither organic nor biodynamic viticulture allows the use of synthetic fungicides, herbicides or pesticides. Organic growers in some major wine-producing countries in Europe such as France, Greece, Hungary, Italy and Portugal solve this problem by using Bordeaux mixture instead, mainly as a fungicide for downy mildew. Bordeaux mixture is comprised of lime, copper sulphate and water. Over time, usage of this mixture can cause copper build-up in vineyards, and so the permitted amounts allowed by the European Commission have been reduced in recent years and it has even been banned in Great Britain and certain parts of Europe. It seems highly dubious whether Bordeaux mixture is any better for the environment than targeted pesticides, although a notable advantage is that it does not penetrate the vine so doesn't leave any residue in the wine.

Sustainable wines

Sustainable winemaking aims to protect the environment by reducing chemical use in the vineyard, whilst also addressing all elements of production in order to reduce their carbon footprint. Practices include using lighter glass bottles, planting trees to offset carbon omissions and recycling waste water. These approaches have been particularly embraced in New Zealand.

Wine Science: How Different Wines are Made

We've looked at the impact of grape variety on taste and also some elements of how the grapes used to make a bottle of wine are grown; it's now time to consider the impact of what happens in the winery.

The role of yeasts

CULTURED VS WILD

Yeasts are arguably the most important part of the whole winemaking process as they are responsible for turning the sugars in the grapes into alcohol (aka fermentation) – so without them there would be no wine! Prior to fermentation the winemaker will have decided if cultured (added) or wild (natural) yeasts will be used. Cultured yeasts are by far the norm, whereas wild fermentations are more artisan as they are less predictable but add complexity to the wine. If you see 'wild ferment' on a label, this is what it means.

SUR LIE

Dead yeast cells tend to drop to the bottom of the fermentation vessel where they form a sediment, called lees. With whites that are quite neutral in flavour and light in structure, the winemaker might leave the wine on this sediment, to add a bit more body and interest to it. This process is called *sur lie*, or 'on the lees'. Lees stirring – *bâtonnage* in French – means moving the lees around both to improve the mouthfeel or texture of the wine and to avoid off flavours.

The fermentation vessel

The majority of fermentation vessels are made from inert materials such as stainless steel, concrete tanks or amphorae, which means they impart no flavour to the wine. However, you'll likely have heard the word 'oaky' applied to the aroma and/or taste of a wine. This means that it has come into contact with oak – usually barrels – during fermentation and/or maturation (ageing) which interacts with the wine, adding flavour.

These oak barrels are typically made from French, Eastern European or American trees, and the woods tend to have different pore sizes, which contribute subtly different tastes to the wine, with French imparting spicier notes such as nutmeg and cinnamon, while American oak imbues sweeter notes of coconut and vanilla. In terms of taste, Eastern European oak is closer to French oak but costs less. Because oak barrels are so expensive, sometimes staves or chips are used to impart an oaky taste to a wine without the cost and investment of a coopered barrel. Barrels and staves can also be charred – or 'toasted' – which will again subtly influence the taste, with more toast equating to more flavour. Oak flavours diminish each time the barrels are re-used, with new oak or 'first fill' having more flavour than second, third fill and each subsequent fill. Ultimately old oak ends up becoming inert and imparting no flavour.

DID YOU KNOW? The vast majority of premium wines fermented and/or matured in oak use French oak because it is subtler. A notable exception to this is Rioja, with American oak accounting for those delicious notes of vanilla and dill, though increasingly, more modern styles of Rioja use a combination of both French and American.

The importance of MLF

Once the alcoholic fermentation is complete, the wine may go through a bacterial conversion called the malolactic fermentation (MLF). Confusingly, this isn't actually a fermentation at all but when, through the action of bacteria, harsh malic acid (think apples) is converted into softer, lactic acid (think milk). Lactic acid produces diacetyl, and it is this that accounts for the buttery taste and soft mouthfeel of some wines. Zingy, fresh whites – such as those found on the Green Fruits & Grass branch of the Tree – are unlikely to go through MLF, while the vast majority of softer whites and even sparkling wines usually do. Most reds go through MLF as a matter of course.

> **REMEMBER** MLF is a bacterial conversion, not a fermentation, that converts harsh malic acid (apples) to softer lactic acid (milk), creating a buttery flavour and a soft mouthfeel.

Additives

Anything that is **added** to the must or juice during the winemaking process is an additive, even the cultured yeasts that are usually employed to kick-start alcoholic fermentation. It is not uncommon to use other additives when making wine too – to facilitate the process and to ensure that the wine is in pristine condition when it arrives on the shelf. Sulphur, tannin, acidity, sugar (added either before fermentation to 'chaptalise' the wine – raise the alcohol content – or after fermentation to sweeten it – *dosage*), calcium carbonate (to de-acidify) and di-ammonium phosphate (a yeast nutrient that helps to keep the yeasts alive and happy during fermentation) may all be used. As we have also seen, oak chips and staves might be added to a wine to impart the flavour of oak. Finally, fining agents may be used to clarify or clean the wine (see below), such as egg whites, casein (a milk protein), or gelatine.

From late 2023, all wines produced for sale in the European Union have to make any ingredients or additives that have gone into the wine accessible to the consumer either by stating them on the label or making them scannable via a QR code.

What is clarification?

When a wine is ready to be bottled, it needs to be made clear and bright, which is known as clarification. This typically involves fining and filtration. Fining is when a fining agent – such as bentonite (clay) – is added to the wine and bonds with floating particles, producing larger ones, which are then easier to remove, while filtration can capture microscopic elements such as yeast. A small amount of the preservative sulphur dioxide (also a natural by-product of fermentation) is usually added at this stage to avoid spoilage or oxidation. Exposure to oxygen can prematurely age or discolour a wine.

How different styles of wine are made:
white, orange, pink and red

This process varies significantly according to the colour of the wine, because it is in the skins of the grapes, rather than the flesh, that both colour and tannins are found. For white wines, neither colour nor tannin is desirable, whereas for red wines they are essential.

WHITE WINEMAKING

HARVEST
▼
CRUSH & PRESS
▼
SETTLE
▼
FERMENT
▼
OPTIONS (MLF, AGEING/MATURATION, BLENDING, ETC.)
▼
CLARIFY
▼
BOTTLE
●

The grapes are harvested either by hand (as whole bunches) or by machine and are then crushed and pressed to release the all-important juice. After a period of settling, where the juice rests to allow unwanted particles to fall to the bottom, it is then moved to a fermentation vessel. Stainless steel tanks are temperature controlled so fermentation is easy to manipulate, and this is ideal for fresh, fruit-forward styles of wine where no oak flavour is wanted. Egg-shaped concrete vessels or clay amphorae are other options, with the 'eggs' emulating the ancient amphorae. Fermentation lasts for an average of fourteen days and, once it is complete, decisions need to be made about whether the wine will go through MLF, if it will be blended with other parcels of wine, and whether to mature the wine in oak.

While white wines are not fermented with their skins, orange wines are. The latter essentially start life as white wines (as they are made from white grapes) but contact with the skins both before, during and sometimes even after fermentation accounts for their enhanced colour.

ORANGE WINEMAKING

HARVEST

CRUSH (AND SOMETIMES PRE-FERMENTATION MACERATION)

FERMENT

POST-FERMENTATION MACERATION

PRESS

OPTIONS (MLF, AGEING/MATURATION, BLENDING, ETC.)

CLARIFY

BOTTLE

Orange (amber or skin-contact) wines are usually dry and made from white grapes when the juice remains in contact with the skins both during and after fermentation, and sometimes even before. This gives the wines a deeper, more orange hue than white wines, and the extra time in contact with the skins makes the wines more textured, tannic and grippy. They are typically fermented in clay fermentation vessels rather than stainless steel tanks or oak barrels. Turn to p. 208 of the autumn section of the book for more information on this fascinating style.

ROSÉ WINEMAKING

HARVEST

▼

CRUSH

▼

SKIN CONTACT

▼

PRESS

▼

SETTLE

▼

FERMENT

▼

CLARIFY

▼

BOTTLE

●

Pink or rosé wine starts life being made like a red wine; the black (also called red) grapes are crushed and the juice is left in contact with the skins until the desired hue of pink is achieved. The juice is then removed and fermented like a white wine, usually with a cool, temperature-controlled fermentation taking place in a stainless steel tank to retain the delicate aromas. The *saignée* method of making rosé wine is when some juice is removed at the very early stages of making red wine, when the liquid has barely had time to take on any colour. This serves not only to produce pink wine, but also to concentrate the remaining must. The rosé that is produced is more like a by-product of red winemaking.

For pink champagne, local red wine (usually Pinot Noir) is typically added to the white blend prior to the secondary fermentation – the one that creates the mousse (or bubbles).

The *saignée* method
of making rosé wine is when
some juice is removed at the very
early stages of making red wine,
when the liquid has barely had
time to take on any colour. This
serves not only to produce pink
wine, but also to concentrate
the remaining must.

RED WINEMAKING

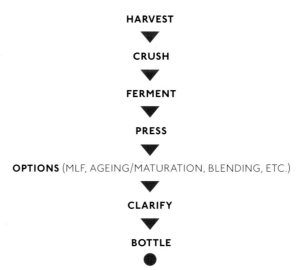

HARVEST

▼

CRUSH

▼

FERMENT

▼

PRESS

▼

OPTIONS (MLF, AGEING/MATURATION, BLENDING, ETC.)

▼

CLARIFY

▼

BOTTLE

●

The crucial difference between red and white winemaking is that in the former the skins need to remain in contact with the juice, because it is the skins that provide the all-important colour and tannins. So for white wines the grapes are pressed and the skins removed; for reds, the grapes are crushed but the skins retained.

Red wines are fermented with their skins:

skins + seeds + stems + juice = must

During red wine fermentation, keeping the skins submerged is crucial to ensure that colour and tannin leach out. This can be done either through 'pumping over' – pumping the must back over the skins that float to the top of the ferment – or 'punching down' – punching the cap of skins back down into the fermenting liquid. Either way, the extraction of both colour and tannins is carefully controlled. Wines that have a lot of colour and are quite tannic tend to be full-bodied and full of rich, dark flavours and are therefore found at the top of the Wine Flavour Tree.

Once fermentation is finished, the higher quality 'free run' wine is removed (or 'racked') from the skins into a clean vessel and the remaining skins are pressed. The winemaker can then blend in some of this press wine later if desired. The wine then undergoes malolactic fermentation, is aged, (possibly) blended, clarified and finally bottled. Some red wines, such as Rioja, will then spend some time ageing in the bottle.

VEGAN AND VEGETARIAN WINE

Towards the end of the winemaking process, wines are usually fined to remove tiny particles that might otherwise make them hazy or bitter. Some premium wines are not fined and, if so, this is usually stated on the bottle. In consequence unfined reds are likely to throw a deposit and so decanting or careful pouring are required to remove any sediment. Wines are fined using a fining agent, and there are a number to choose from. They include bentonite, which is a type of clay, egg whites (or albumen), casein (derived from milk), isinglass (fish bladders) and gelatine (derived from animal bones, cartilage and skin). Vegetarian wine production excludes the use of isinglass and gelatine, while vegan winemaking additionally rejects the use of egg whites or casein.

LOW OR 'NO ADDED SULPHUR' WINE

Sulphur dioxide is a natural by-product of the fermentation process and yet winemakers usually add more prior to bottling because it is an antioxidant – it prevents the wine from spoiling and going brown, which is especially noticeable in white wines. It is also a preservative and prevents the growth of unwanted yeast or bacteria. Because sulphites can be an allergen, 'contains sulphites' has to be written on the label of any wine that contains over ten parts per million. Sulphur tends to get the rap for hangovers and headaches, though the culprit for both is far more likely to be the alcohol itself. A bag of dried apricots contains more sulphur than a bottle of wine, and no one complains of a hangover after eating dried fruit!

DID YOU KNOW? Some individuals, however, do actually have an intolerance to sulphur dioxide and should look out for low or no added sulphur wines, where sulphur dioxide has been added either in very small amounts or not at all. Wine intolerance (headaches that aren't a hangover) can also be caused by histamines, another natural by-product of fermentation. Taking an antihistamine prior to wine consumption can help.

NATURAL WINES

Since all wines are made from grapes, a natural product, it could be deduced that all wines are natural. However, some are deemed to be more natural than others. Natural wines are made from organic or biodynamically grown grapes, harvested by hand, and made with as little human intervention as possible. The wines therefore use wild rather than cultured yeasts and fermentation is not assisted but allowed to run its course naturally. No additives are used, with sulphur being the only exception, and if it is, only in tiny amounts – far lower than is allowed for conventional wines. The wines are also not fined or filtered and as a consequence can be a little 'funky', hazy or even sour, but the best have astonishing purity of fruit. Buying natural wines therefore can be a bit of a lottery, especially as some may re-ferment. This is a risk which comes from not adding sulphur coupled with no fining or filtering, as the yeasts remain in the wine and can cause problems if they are dormant rather than dead.

Currently the term 'natural wine' has no official meaning outside France. There, to qualify as a *vin méthode nature*, a wine must contain no additives, be made from hand-harvested, certified organic grapes and sulphur has to be kept to a minimum – below thirty milligrams per litre. Wines with no added sulphur can add the words '*sans sulfites ajoutés*' under the logo.

DID YOU KNOW? The majority of orange wines are actually natural; they typically use the centuries-old traditional Georgian way of winemaking, which is extremely low intervention in its philosophy. However, if they are fined, filtered or if cultured yeasts or too much sulphur has been added, then they aren't.

OTHER TYPES OF WINE

- Sparkling (see pp. 126–35)
- Fortified & sweet (see pp. 254–62)

EVERYTHING YOU NEED TO KNOW ABOUT WINE TASTING

A really fascinating thing about wine tasting is that the most important part of the experience isn't the taste of wine, but the smell. There are actually only five tastes that can be detected on the tongue by the tastebuds and these are sweet, salty, bitter, sour and umami. It is when taste – what is perceived on the tongue – is combined with aroma that the flavour of wine is experienced.

Interestingly, most of the smell of a wine occurs inside the mouth, retronasally, as the aromas travel from the back of the mouth and up the olfactory passage – which is inside the nose – rather than orthonasally, which is when an aroma is smelled outside the body, via the nostrils. Taste therefore is only experienced when whatever is put in the mouth, be it wine, a piece of cheese or a chocolate, reacts with the tastebuds – specifically the taste receptor cells that are located there – and is felt as a sensation on the tongue. Flavour is more complex as it is determined by both taste and smell, with the aroma rather than the taste of wine being the fundamental and dominant factor. Crucially therefore, when it comes to enjoying wine, we are not really wine tasting, we are wine smelling.

REMEMBER The most important part of the experience isn't the taste of the wine, but the smell!

1.

SEE

The colour of a wine can give a really good indication as to what grape variety it is made from as well as its provenance and even its age, so take a good look.

2.

SWIRL

Next, swirl the wine gently around the glass as this lets air in and allows for the release of those crucial aromas.

HOW TO TASTE WINE

3.

SNIFF

As you don't really wine-taste, you wine-smell, 'nosing' a wine is an integral part of wine tasting so take your time. Short, sharp sniffs are better.

4.

SIP

Now draw some wine into the mouth through the lips (ideally along with some air), so that you can taste and continue to assess the wine.

How to 'Taste' Wine for Ultimate Enjoyment

It's a really good idea to follow a few simple steps when tasting a wine and after a while these will become more natural and eventually, second nature. The most important part of this process is to make it easier for you to smell the volatile aromas in the wine and so, before you start, pour only a modest amount into your glass – about four centimetres. This means that you you can really get the air in and swirl it around without it going everywhere!

The four basic steps are:

1. **SEE:** The colour of a wine can give a really good indication as to what grape variety it is made from as well as its provenance and even its age, so take a good look.
2. **SWIRL:** Next, swirl the wine gently around the glass as this lets air in and allows for the release of those crucial aromas.
3. **SNIFF:** As you don't really wine-taste, you wine-smell, 'nosing' a wine is an integral part of wine tasting so take your time. Short, sharp sniffs are better.
4. **SIP:** Now draw some wine into the mouth through the lips (ideally along with some air), so that you can taste and continue to assess the wine.

TIP With all commercial and fine wines, you want to make sure that the wine looks clean and bright with no haze or cloudiness, as this would indicate the presence of unwanted yeast or bacteria, which is a fault. However, many natural wines are unfined and unfiltered, which can result in a slight haze.

STEP 1 – SEE

Once you've poured some wine into your glass, the first thing to do is to look at it, as the colour of the wine really does provide some crucial information about what is in front of you.

For white wines:

- The lighter the colour, the more likely it is that the wine is very young and/or unoaked, and/or from a cooler climate and/or from a light-bodied grape variety such as Garganega (the Soave grape) or Sauvignon Blanc.
- A white that is golden in colour might be more mature, and/or richer and fuller and/or oaked and/or from a warmer climate, with riper fruit flavours, such as those found in a Chardonnay or Viognier, with the resultant viscosity, structure and alcohol.

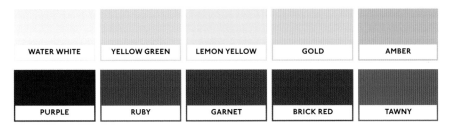

With red wines, the colour is also important and is usually a good indicator of age:

- Vivid purple indicates a very young wine.
- Brick or tawny hints at significant bottle age.

As with white wines, colour is also linked to grape variety:

- Grapes with thick skins (especially those with small berries) tend to produce wines with more colour and tannins, such as Cabernet Sauvignon.
- Grapes with large berries and thin skins, such as Pinot Noir, tend to produce wines lighter in colour.

So, here is a short summary of what the colour of the wine can tell you:

- It hints both at the provenance of the wine and the grape variety.
- The depth and the colour of the wine can also give an indication as to its age. If a wine's colour lies on the right-hand side of the chart on p. 55, it is likely to be older: deeper golden and amber colours for whites and brick-red or tawny colours for reds. Bright purple and ruby hues tend to suggest younger red wines and the colour of a young white is generally water-white through to gold.
- The colour and clarity can tell you if the wine is faulty. Wine should be clean and bright with no hazes. A really golden colour coupled with a smell of sherry might mean that the wine is oxidised; that it has spoiled due to unintentional exposure to air.

WINE FACT Tiny crystals in the wine might look alarmingly like shards of glass but are only tartrate crystals (sometimes called wine diamonds), formed when the wine has been exposed to cold temperatures and not been cold-stabilised prior to bottling. Sediment is also harmless, though it does mean that the wine would benefit from being carefully decanted.

STEP 2 – SWIRL

You are now ready to get swirling. When I first went into the wine trade I thought this looked rather pretentious (don't even get me started on when I first saw people spitting wine!), but given that, as mentioned, you wine-smell rather than wine-taste, this step really does help with the whole 'tasting experience'. This will get easier with practice.

Hold your glass by the stem – this gives you greater control and also stops you from warming up the wine too much if it's white or rosé – and then gently move the glass rhythmically in a circular fashion so that the wine gently moves around inside the glass. I swirl anti-clockwise and you need do it for only a matter of seconds, say around five. Swirling increases the wine's exposure to the air, which in turn increases the rate at which the aroma molecules contained within it volatilise – this makes the wine easier to smell.

DID YOU KNOW? You don't actually need to swirl sparkling wine because the bubbles inside the wine help release the aromas for you and repeated swirling will only make your wine flat.

STEP 3 – SNIFF

From bonfires to baked bread, it is amazing the huge number of aromas the brain has filed away in its memory bank. More than any of our other senses, smell is intrinsically linked to memory, which is why we are better at recognising smells that we come across often and which are quite distinctive. Recognising certain smells can also be useful for self-preservation, from detecting smoke to the just-off smell of raw meat. When tasting wine, we swirl before sniffing to release those all-important volatile aromatics for our nasal receptors to capture so that our brains can then translate them into something we recognise.

The time has now come to try to identify some aromas, so turn back to the Wine Flavour Tree, look up the grape variety that is in your glass, gently swirl it and . . . sniff! Hopefully you will be able to detect some of the aroma icons on the relevant branch.

TIP Our noses start to tire after six seconds so it is better to take lots of short sniffs rather than a long one.

FRUIT VS FAULT

Besides trying to identify the aromas in your glass, you also need to check that it is 'clean', which means that it's not faulty in any way. The main fault you are checking for is whether the wine is 'corked'. Rather than a wine having pieces of cork in it from poor extraction, this is when the cork has a taint called TCA (or 2,4,6-trichloroanisole), which is transferred to the wine and makes it smell to varying degrees dusty, cardboardy or mouldy. There are other faults to look for out for too, such as the aforementioned oxidation, but the main culprit is cork, so that is the most important one to try to get a handle on. This is the reason why a sommelier in a restaurant gives you the wine to check – you are confirming the wine isn't faulty, rather than that you like it.

TIP Don't smell the cork itself to see if the wine is corked: smell the wine! I have seen corks that look mouldy and vile beyond belief but the wine is clean as a whistle, but also pristine, gorgeous corks with no apparent taint yet the wine is rank.

STEP 4 – SIP

Now that you've smelled your wine and hopefully identified an aroma or two, you're ready to taste what is in your glass. In part, you're just checking what your nose has already told you, which is why when tasting it's a good idea to take a small amount of wine into your mouth, hold it there, purse your lips and then softly pull some air in through them. By doing this you're essentially repeating the swirling step, but in your mouth rather than a glass. The air drawn in through your lips carries the volatile aromas up the olfactory passage from your mouth to your brain. Don't gargle the wine – it shouldn't go to the back of your throat until you are ready to swallow it. Keep it in your mouth, where your tastebuds will (hopefully) be enjoying the wine, but also assessing its structure and flavour.

Wine tasting cheat sheet

Personally, I find thinking about the structure of a wine far easier than identifying aromas. You are trying to detect and determine:

- **ACIDITY** The best way to try to identify the acidity in a wine and decide whether it is low, medium or high is to think about citrus fruits. These are all fairly acidic (they have a low pH), which is why they make your mouth water. If a wine really makes your mouth water and is quite tart and lemony then it has high acidity, moderate if less so and finally low if the acidity is not especially perceptible.
- **ALCOHOL** This is felt at the back of the mouth and is best described as a warming sensation; the higher the alcohol the more 'heat' will be detected. However, if the wine is in balance, even if it has a fairly high level of alcohol (I'd say anything over 14–14.5 per cent by volume), you shouldn't notice any alcohol 'burn'.
- **TANNINS** These are responsible for a drying sensation felt at the sides of the mouth (like when drinking strong tea) and are found pretty much exclusively in red wines. Excessive tannins can make a wine seem bitter and dry, as can unripe tannins, which also have a green, stalky flavour to them. Ripe tannins help make a wine seem supple and smooth.

You also want to assess:

- **BODY** The weight or body of a wine is usually described as light, medium or full, and is felt in the middle of the tongue. Think skimmed, semi-skimmed and full-fat milk; texturally they have different viscosities and respectively feel watery, medium in weight or rich and creamy.
- **SWEETNESS** This is detected on the tip of the tongue and is different to fruit ripeness – sometimes the two can be confused. A wine can seem really ripe, fruity and flavourful, but that does not mean it is sweet.

Ripeness and fruit are detected in the mid-palate as opposed to on the tip of the tongue. The vast majority of commercially available wines are dry.

- **OAK FLAVOURS** Oak in wine can be detected both by its flavours and by the structure it imparts. Flavourwise, French (and European) oak is like a sprinkling of spice (nutmeg or cinnamon mainly), while American contributes dill, vanilla and/or coconut. Structurally, oak is felt as tannins in the mouth in the same way as the wine tannins – at the sides, like tea.

At this point, it's also a good idea to think back to BLIC – Balance, Length, Intensity, Complexity. Are all the components of the wine (acidity, alcohol, tannins and so on) in balance? Does it have good length – can you taste it for a long time once you have swallowed it? Is there enough intensity – depth of fruit on the mid-palate? And is it interesting and multi-layered – complexity?

   When all is said and done, however, the most important thing to decide when you taste a wine is whether you like it or not.

HOW TO FIND THE BEST BOTTLE FOR YOU, ON ANY BUDGET

How to Understand a Wine Label: Varietal vs Regional Labelling

A NOTE ABOUT TERMINOLOGY

For years it has been common parlance to talk about either 'Old World' or 'New World' wines. Historically this encapsulated both the geographical origin of a wine but also tradition, climate and attitude, with 'traditional' winemaking methods being associated with the Old World and 'modern' with the New. Increasingly this feels rather outdated – certainly taking into account the colonial connotations of the terms – and so even though they are not perfect, I will be using 'Classic European', 'Other European' and 'Rest of the World' instead (see p. 65 for a table).

Classic European: Many countries with a long history of making wine, certainly those with numerous 'fine wine' regions – such as France, Italy and Spain – label their wines according to that region, sub-region, village or even vineyard. In France for example, wines from Burgundy, Bordeaux and the Rhône bear the name of the region on the label, rather than the grape they are made from, though no one country uses regional labelling exclusively.

Other European: These countries may have a long history of making wine (such as Georgia, Germany and Portugal) and also be governed by strict rules and regulations but their wines are largely labelled varietally not regionally.

Rest of the World: The Southern Hemisphere and the United States where wines are labelled varietally.

Given that one of the main reasons a wine tastes the way that it does is the grape variety or varieties used to make it, it is entirely logical to look for that information on the label when choosing your wine; it's simply the quickest way to understand what it's likely to taste like. Unfortunately it's not that straightforward.

Wines from Classic European countries are predominantly labelled by where they are made, exclusively so in some famous regions. Often there is no mention of the grape variety at all, on either the front or the back label. This is because certain grape varieties have been grown in different regions for centuries, and over time it has become clear what varieties flourish where. As a result it is only those specific grapes that are allowed to be grown in those regions by law – thus becoming synonymous with each other. For example, white Sancerre (Sancerre being a small town or *ville* in the Loire Valley, France) can only ever be made from the Sauvignon Blanc grape. If a white wine were to be made in Sancerre from a different grape variety (which is highly unlikely to happen for this very reason!), it couldn't legally be called Sancerre. Champagne can only come from the Champagne region of France, and Italian Barolo can only be made from the Nebbiolo grape. These cast-iron wine laws exist to protect the region, the quality of the wines and the consumer.

Conversely the Other European and Rest of the World countries tend to label their wines varietally, which is to say that the grape(s) from which the wine was made, such as Chardonnay, Grüner Veltliner, Malbec, Riesling or Shiraz, are given centre stage on the label. This makes it SO much easier for the wine consumer to navigate their way around buying a bottle of wine because the grape variety – and hence the likely taste of the wine

– is clearly shown. The region does still have to appear on the label but with the grape variety, not instead of.

Other useful bits of information that can be found on the front label might include the vintage (this is the year in which the grapes were picked), the country of origin and the name of the producer or winery. The back label tends to carry a description of the wine, the alcohol content and other legal requirements.

DID YOU KNOW? Most of the popular international grape varieties are indigenous to – and therefore have their origins in – France. From Syrah (also known as Shiraz, especially in Australia), to Merlot, Pinot Noir, Cabernet Sauvignon, Cabernet Franc, Pinot Gris (known as Pinot Grigio in Italy), Gamay, Chenin Blanc, Viognier, Sémillon and Malbec, they are all French! Tempranillo and Garnacha (known as Grenache in France and elsewhere) are Spanish, Riesling is German and Nebbiolo and Sangiovese are Italian. The different grape varieties were then taken around the world from their birthplaces and are now found in most wine producing countries.

CLASSIC EUROPEAN COUNTRIES	OTHER EUROPEAN COUNTRIES	REST OF THE WORLD
France	Austria *	Argentina
Italy	Bulgaria	Australia
Spain	Croatia	Canada
	Georgia **	Chile
	Germany *	Lebanon
	Greece **	New Zealand
	Hungary **	South Africa
	Portugal ***	United States
	Romania	Uruguay
	Switzerland	
	Turkey	
	Ukraine	
	United Kingdom	

* Austria and Germany are in 'Other European' because even though they have a long history of winemaking and strict wine laws, rules and regulations, their wines are labelled varietally.

** Georgia, Greece and Hungary all have a long history of winemaking but are also in 'Other European' because their wines tend to be labelled varietally (minus Tokaji).

*** Portugal is in 'Other European' because while it has a long history of port production, its success with unfortified table wines is far more recent.

VARIETAL VS REGIONAL LABELLING IN PRACTICE

The first label is from a fictitious producer – 'The Mistress of Wine' – based in New Zealand and is therefore labelled varietally, with the front label clearly showing the name of the grape as well as the producer, the vintage, the region and country. Labels like this go a long way to explaining the popularity of wines like New Zealand Sauvignon Blanc – along with the exuberant nature of them stylistically – both when they first came on to the market and still today, because the grape information is clearly stated on the label and so wine selection is straightforward.

THE MISTRESS OF WINE

Sauvignon Blanc
Malborough, New Zealand
2024

Compare this to the second label, which is typical of a wine from a Classic European country – France – and a fine wine region within that – Sancerre – and so has to be labelled regionally: often the grape variety can't even be found on the back label.

Domaine Caporn

2023

SANCERRE

Appellation Sancerre Contrôlée

Mis en bouteille au Domaine
Caporn Sancerre France

The front label shows the name of the producer – Domaine Caporn – the vintage (2023), region and country of origin (France), but it does not show the grape variety. When buying wines from Classic European countries, therefore, a certain amount of wine knowledge is required in order to understand 'what is grown where' aka regional labelling and thus know what you are purchasing (in this case white Sancerre = Sauvignon Blanc). When it comes to determining what grape variety is in the bottle, the onus therefore is really on the consumer.

WINES AND THEIR GRAPES

This table shows some examples of wines from Classic European countries that are labelled regionally and what grapes they are permitted to be made from.

REGION ON THE LABEL

Amarone (Veneto, Italy)

Barolo and Barbaresco (Piedmont, Italy)

Beaujolais (east-central France)

Bordeaux (left bank of the Gironde Estuary, France)

Bordeaux (right bank of the Gironde Estuary, France)

Brunello di Montelcino (Tuscany, Italy)

Chablis (Burgundy, France)

Châteauneuf-du-Pape (southern Rhône, France)

Chianti (Tuscany, Italy)

Chinon (Loire, France)

Condrieu (Rhône, France)

Cornas (Rhône, France)

Côte de Beaune (Burgundy, France, part of the Côte d'Or)

Côte de Nuits (Burgundy, France, part of the Côte d'Or)

Côte de Provence (Provence, France)

Gevrey-Chambertin and other Côte d'Orreds (Burgundy, France)

Puligny-Montrachet and other Côte d'Or whites (Burgundy, France)

Ribera del Duero (Castilla y León, Spain)

Rioja (La Rioja, Spain)

Sancerre (Loire, France)

Sancerre (Loire, France)

Soave (Veneto, Italy)

Toro (Castilla y León, Spain)

Valpolicella (Verona, Italy)

PERMITTED GRAPE VARIETIES

Predominantly Corvina (red)

Nebbiolo (red)

Gamay (red)

Usually a Cabernet Sauvignon-dominated blend (red)

Usually a Merlot-dominated blend (red)

Sangiovese (red)

Chardonnay (white)

Grenache noir-based blend (red) and Grenache blanc-based blend (white)

Predominantly Sangiovese (red)

Cabernet Franc (red)

Viognier (white)

Syrah (red)

Chardonnay (white), Pinot Noir (red)

Pinot Noir (red), Chardonnay (white)

92 per cent rosé (blends, mainly red grapes)

Pinot Noir (red)

Chardonnay (white)

Tinto Fino aka Tempranillo (red)

Predominantly Tempranillo (red)

Sauvignon Blanc (white)

Pinot Noir (red)

Garganega (white)

Predominantly Tinta de Toro aka Tempranillo (red)

Corvina (red)

Classic European and Other European wine laws

Wine production in the Classic European countries and many of the Other European ones – such as Austria, Germany and Portugal – is governed (aside from the European Union) by their own individual and fairly complex wine laws. These encompass the permitted grape variety or varieties and other areas such as yield and production methods. But arguably the most important part of these laws is that which pertains to the quality levels of the wines and this is always stated on the label. On our Sancerre label, for example, the words 'Appellation Sancerre Contrôlée' can be seen, as under the French system this wine falls into the top 'AOC' classification: Appellation d'Origine Contrôlée.

The rest of the world

The Rest of the World – which includes countries in both the northern and the southern hemispheres – also has rules in place that differ slightly by country, but generally speaking they are not as stringent as in European countries, especially the Classic ones. A key requirement, for example, includes ensuring that when a single grape variety is shown on the label, that variety accounts for a minimum percentage of the wine in that bottle. In the United States, Australia and New Zealand, if the label shows the wine is a Sauvignon Blanc, for example, 85 per cent of that wine has to be Sauvignon. That figure reduces to 75 per cent in South Africa and Chile, but in Argentina it is 100 per cent.

At a glance: how to spot wine quality

Here are some of the most important European classifications organised from highest to lowest quality. Please note however that excellent wines can be made at all levels: think of the Super Tuscans – extremely high-quality red wines made in Tuscany in the 1970s, but with non-indigenous varieties, so they had to be declassified and sold as lowly Vino do Tavola – or innovative producers today who are pushing the envelope stylistically but making wines that don't adhere to their country's strict quality system.

FRANCE

- Highest – AOC (Appellation d'Origine Contrôlée), the same thing as the Europe-wide PDO (Protected Designation of Origin) or AOP (Appellation d'Origine Protégée) in French. Some of the larger and more famous regions such as Bordeaux, Burgundy and Champagne also have further classifications to watch out for on the label, such as Grand Cru, Premier Cru and Grand Cru Classé.
- Medium – IGP (Indication Géographique Protégée). These wines were formerly classified as Vin de Pays.
- Lowest – Vin de France

> **DID YOU KNOW?** If a vintage is mentioned on a label then the wine is 100 per cent from that vintage. Specific regional rules will dictate if wines are single varietals or blends.

ITALY

- Highest – DOCG (Denominazione di Origine Controllata e Garantita), the European DOP (Denominazione di Origine Protetta) which includes Barolo and Chianti
- High – DOC (Denominazione di Origine Controllata), also DOP
- Medium – IGP (Indicazione Geografica Protetta)
- Lowest – Vino da Tavola

SPAIN

Within the DOP (Denominación de Origen Protegida) category there are:

- Highest – Vino de Pago (VP) or single-estate wines
- High – DOCa (Denominación de Origen Calificada) or DOQ in Catalan and this classification is restricted to Rioja and Priorat
- DO (Denominación de Origen)
- Medium – VC (Vinos de Calidad) – the lowest level of DOP wines
- Low – IGP (Indicación Geográfica Protegida) – these used to be called Vino de la Tierra or VT and can still use that name
- Lowest – Vino de Mesa

PORTUGAL

- Highest – DOC (Denominação de Origem Controlada), the European DOP (Denominação de Origem Protegida)
- Medium – IGP (Indicação Geográfica Protegida) or Vinho Regional
- Lowest – Vinho

GERMANY

- Highest – Prädikatswein. Within this class there are six ripeness levels, determined according to the must weights or sugar in the grapes. These range from Kabinett (typically the lightest) through Spätlese, Auslese, Beerenauslese and Eiswein (the same must weight as Beerenauslese but made from frozen grapes) to Trockenbeerenauslese. The latter three are always sweet.
- Highest – Qualitätswein or PDO in Germany. The grapes have to come from one of Germany's thirteen wine regions. The VDP (Verband Deutscher Prädikatsweingüter) is a national growers' organisation of around 200 wine estates that represent some of the very best of German wines, identified both on the neck of the bottle and label by a logo of an eagle and a bunch of grapes. The best vineyard sites are called Grosse Lage ('great site' or grand cru) or Erste Lage (premier cru) followed by Ortswein and Gutswein. Dry Grosse Lage wines are labelled Grosses Gewächs (GG).
- Medium – Landwein (PGI also called geschützte geographische Angube or g.g.A.)
- Lower – Deutscher Wein

AUSTRIA

- Highest – Qualitätswein. This includes Kabinett, 'regionally typical' Qualitätswein or DAC (Districtus Austriae Controllatus) of which there are currently eighteen permitted regions, Prädikatswein (Spätlese, Auslese, Beerenauslese, Eiswein, Strohwein and Trockenbeerenauslese) and Sekt.
- Medium – Landwein
- Lowest – Wein

Decoding Your Wine Bottle

In some of the Classic and Other European regions, even the shape of the bottle is determined by wine law and this tends to be replicated throughout the Rest of the World, with the bottle shape chosen depending on the grape variety or varieties used. For example, a Pinot Noir that is made in Australia or South Africa will be bottled in a Burgundy-shaped bottle because red Burgundy is made from that grape. Even the bottle itself therefore can provide a clue as to the style of wine that is inside:

ALSACE

The flute bottle is called the Alsace – it is tall and slim and used for aromatic grape varieties such as Riesling, Gewürztraminer and Pinot Gris.

BORDEAUX

The Bordeaux bottle has straight sides and is typically used for grapes like Cabernet Sauvignon, Merlot and Malbec.

From left to right: the bottle shapes used in Alsace, Bordeaux, Burgundy and Champagne.

BURGUNDY

The more curved/sloping Burgundy bottle tends to house varieties such as Chardonnay, Pinot Noir, Grenache, Gamay and Viognier.

CHAMPAGNE

An instantly recognisable bottle is the heavy champagne bottle, needed to withstand the pressure of the bubbles inside.

Cost and Quality

It's really useful to consider the costs involved in producing a bottle of wine for sale so that you know what you're paying for.

First of all, for every bottle of wine – not including the actual cost of the liquid itself or the retailer margin/profit – there are what are called fixed costs. These include the cost of the glass bottle, the cork or closure, the label, shipping, duty and VAT. For a bottle of wine that is bought for around £5, the vast majority of that money goes towards the fixed costs – especially duty and VAT – with very little being left over for the wine itself. Up to a certain point, therefore, the more you spend, the more you are really spending on the wine itself.

The cost of the wine component in the bottle is very much driven by how the wine was made. In the vineyard, was the focus on quantity or quality? If large volumes of fruit were grown on the vine resulting in high yields, then the wine won't be as concentrated, but the cost of growing the grapes can be spread over more bottles and so the wine should be cheaper. If however the emphasis was on growing great grapes for premium wine, then smaller quantities of higher-quality fruit will be produced, sacrificing quantity for quality: therefore the cost will be greater.

The grapes themselves might also have been costly to buy – as in Champagne for example. The vineyards are valuable and therefore the grapes are expensive, coupled with the fact that champagne is also expensive to make, and capital is tied up while the wine is being aged. Marketing and advertising don't come cheap either . . . You can also expect to pay more for wines that have been fermented or matured in oak as barrels are expensive and, similarly to champagne, ageing wines is costly too.

For the majority of wines therefore, I think it is safe to say that, once you put retailer margin aside – which can vary quite significantly – you generally get what you pay for, with pricier wines being more interesting, concentrated and complex as well as displaying a sense of place and varietal purity. When it comes to fine wine, however, some prestigious villages, vineyards and châteaux are small and so can only produce a certain, finite amount of wine. Supply and demand therefore dictates that high prices can be charged for the bottles. The same principle applies to 'cult' or 'icon' wines and wines that are very old and rare. The price of these can be astronomical, with the most expensive wine ever sold being a bottle of red Burgundy; a Domaine de la Romanée-Conti Romanée-Conti Grand Cru 1945 that sold for $558,000 in 2018.

And finally, what about wine promotions; are they worthwhile? The best promotions are indisputably those that occur across an entire range – when retailers run a 25-per-cent-off promotion, for example – and this is an excellent time to go shopping for the wine rack. However, do watch out for excessive price cuts, particularly if they go hand in hand with heavy bottles with deep punts (the big dimple in the bottom) and/or embossed labels, as these tactics are employed to make a wine look more expensive than it really is. You don't tend to see half-price offers around any more, but the wine was usually only worth the promotional price rather than the full bottle price in the first place. Discount retailers are a reliable place to go shopping for good value wines though as they focus on permanent low prices.

SUMMARY:

- **Rule of thumb 1:** Think about the 'fixed costs' of a wine – if you trade up/spend a bit more on a bottle most of your extra money goes towards the quality of the wine itself.
- **Rule of thumb 2:** Lower yields tend to equate to better quality.
- **Rule of thumb 3:** Wines that have been fermented and/or aged in oak barrels will command a premium, but in my opinion, it's worth it (I'm a total oak hound).

Common Wine Faults

When you are asked to taste the wine you have ordered (in a bar, pub or restaurant) you are being asked to confirm that you think the wine is 'clean' – that it's not faulty in any way, and that you are happy to keep it. It's not really about whether you like it or not.

The most important wine fault to be able to recognise is whether a wine is corked or not (see p. 58 for more information). There are varying degrees of corked wine from barely noticeable (the wine might just seem a bit dull) to the truly hideous and unmistakeable smell of mould.

DID YOU KNOW? Very rarely, you can get a corked wine that has been closed with a screw cap! This occurs when the taint is present in the winery, such as in the bottling line.

Another fault is **oxidation**. This is when a wine smells a bit like sherry when it shouldn't. Red wines can taste a bit 'dried out' and whites can go very golden in colour, sometimes even taking on a hint of browning, with a distinct, appley note.

Something that is easy to spot is when a still wine has a bit of spritz or fizz to it when it shouldn't. Here the wine is likely to be **re-fermenting** – this will definitely be the case if the wine is a bit hazy too. Do be aware, though, that some wines, such as the Portuguese Vinho Verde, have a very light intentional *petillance* to them, and some very young wines might also display a tiny prickle on the palate due to the addition of carbon dioxide for freshness.

Brettanomyces is a yeast that affects red wines and at low concentrations can add complexity and interest (notes of spice) but, if there is too much, you might be able to smell or taste a medicinal, calamine-lotion character or even a slightly horsey, stable or farmyard-like aroma. The wines can also appear quite drying and tannic on the finish.

Never buy an expensive bottle of wine stored in a shop window with the sun shining on it, or from the top shelf of an off-licence, sitting under a strip light as it is likely to have been damaged by ultraviolet (UV) light. This is a fairly recent topic in terms of wine faults, but **light strike** can make wines – whites in particular – taste a bit like cabbage. Green rather than clear bottles help to protect the wine.

Finally, **reduction**. This is when there isn't enough oxygen or air in the wine and it can smell a bit sulphury – think matchsticks or even eggs. Decanting the wine to aerate it will help enormously.

Storing and Serving Wine

Storing wine

For those – like myself – who don't have a collection of fine wine, their own cellar, or enough expensive bottles to warrant a third party storing them on their behalf, the main things to remember are that wine doesn't like light, heat or movement/vibrations. For these reasons, storing wine in the kitchen (light and heat) or under the stairs (people thudding up and down) isn't ideal. Another thing to remember is that wines need to be stored horizontally to prevent the corks drying out, if you are planning on ageing them for a few years or more. If the wines are for fairly immediate drinking then this obviously doesn't matter, and ditto if the wine is sparkling – the pressure inside the bottle keeps the cork moist – or if the wine is closed with a screwcap or synthetic cork. It is also worth remembering that smaller bottles age faster than large ones so a half-bottle will evolve faster than a magnum (the equivalent of two bottles of wine).

DID YOU KNOW? Sparkling wines – including champagne – can be stored vertically because the pressure in the bottle keeps the cork moist.

Serving wine

The only thing that really matters when it comes to serving wine is to try to serve a tasty bottle, ideally with seasonal food and good company. However, it is fairly straightforward to enhance the whole experience by paying attention to a few things.

TEMPERATURE

White wines are frequently served too cold and reds too warm. For red wines, room temperature means cellar temperature rather than that of a centrally heated dining room or kitchen. While wine racks can look gorgeous as a feature in your kitchen, they are really not a good idea. Reds that are a little warm can taste 'jammy'; the alcohol becomes more evident and the wine is just not as fresh and drinkable. Personally, I like my white wines to be really quite cold and am happy to compromise a bit on flavour to achieve that, but there is no doubt that as wine warms up in the glass, it becomes more open and aromatically expressive. A great rule to follow is to take your white **out** of the fridge and to pop your red bottle **in**, twenty minutes before you want to drink them.

- For sparkling, light white and rosé wines, the ideal temperature is 5–8°C.
- For fuller bodied whites, more flavourful rosés, lighter reds and pudding wines, 8–13°C.
- For richer reds and fortified wines, 15–20°C maximum.

REMEMBER Take your white wine out of the fridge and pop your red in, twenty minutes before you want to drink them: but as ever, personal preference is key.

GLASSWARE

Glassware undoubtedly affects and can enhance the flavour of wine. For sparkling wine I favour a tulip-shaped glass as opposed to a flute or coupe (even if they do look gorgeous), as a flute is quite narrow, which makes the aroma harder to appreciate, and a coupe glass can allow the fizz to escape too fast. With still wines, I highly recommend using a glass with a stem as it makes the wine so much easier to swirl and it feels more like a treat. I know many prefer stem-free glasses, but I am not one of them.

There are so many different glasses that have been tailored to wines made from particular grape varieties and from specific regions. Many appeared on my wedding gift list and . . . I don't use them. I fall back on my favourite glass, which I use universally for white, red and rosé, and I would suggest that this is the most practical thing to do. The best (but most expensive) wine glass brands are Riedel and Zalto, which both have a universal glass, as does the Richard Brendon Jancis Robinson Collection (and you can use this glass for fizz too).

The thickness of the rim, the heaviness of the glass and the shape of the stem and bowl all influence, to very subtle degrees, what the wine smells and tastes like. They can break very easily, however, so a sensible (and cost-effective) thing to do is to buy a generic red wine glass and use that as your universal glass. Make sure it isn't too chunky and is intended for medium- to full-bodied wines, to make sure there is enough space in the glass for a really good swirl.

TIP I know it's a pain, but I wash my wine glasses by hand and give them a really good rinse to make sure there's no detergent left on the glass. One of the best investments I have ever made was a wine-glass drying rack; they might take up a bit of space and aren't necessarily beautiful but they are brilliant!

DECANTING

There are two fundamental reasons to decant wine: to remove the wine from any sediment or deposit and to allow the wine to 'breathe' or 'open up' by oxygenating it. It is usually red wines that are unfined, older or fortified such as vintage port that throw a deposit. Remember, as these wines age, the tannins bind together into long chains that then become too heavy and break – called polymerisation – which causes the sediment. To remove wine from its sediment, pour the liquid through some muslin, a coffee filter or my favourite – a pop sock – and into a decanter, leaving the sediment behind in the material. If you want to return the wine to its original bottle, then just rinse it and pour the wine back in. This is known as double decanting.

TIP You don't need fancy accessories; a decanter can simply be a jug.

Decanting a wine to aerate it pretty much improves any and every wine – not just expensive wines – from sparkling to white and red, though it is usually only done for the latter. The simple act of pouring wine out of its bottle and into another receptacle allows air into the wine and ultimately makes it softer and easier to smell and taste. Care needs to be taken when decanting very old wine, however, as it will be more fragile and the air can make the fruit fade faster, so you wouldn't want to leave it in the decanter for very long, arguably for no longer than half an hour. Young, full-bodied reds benefit the most from decanting and can easily be left for a couple of hours in a decanter to open up.

OPENING A BOTTLE OF WINE

When opening a bottle of sparkling wine make sure that the bottle is sufficiently chilled (this really helps control the fizz!) and that once the foil and wire muzzle are removed you never take your hand off the unsecured cork. Finally, twist the bottle and NOT the cork. This should allow you to open the bottle with the equivalent of a whisper rather than a more exuberant pop. For still wines it is far simpler; either twist a screwcap, or remove the foil and then the cork, using a corkscrew. Older corks can also be tricky as they can crumble so take care. I find a simple waiter's friend corkscrew the most reliable and if the cork does break in two, don't panic, just crack on with removing the remaining segment. If you really struggle then push the cork into the bottle and decant. Ditto if you have cork dust or particles in the wine, just decant to clean it up.

> **TIP** I find wax tops to be a bit of a pain but they don't actually need to be removed. Because they aren't that thick, just drive the corkscrew through the wax seal, pull and extract along with the cork.

HOW LONG CAN YOU LEAVE WINE ONCE OPENED?

The best way to preserve *any* wine that has been opened but not finished is to pop the cork back in and put it in the fridge. A champagne or sparkling wine bottle stopper is an excellent, small investment and, although I don't use one, wine vacuum pumps are a great way to remove the air from the headspace of an opened bottle of still wine. Air is the enemy of wine, so the emptier the bottle the more air is inside and the faster it will spoil. If you have less than half a bottle of wine, an alternative to a vacuum pump is to pour any unfinished wine into an empty half-bottle (hang on to a clean, empty one for this purpose), pop the cork back in and put the wine in the fridge. When it comes to sparkling wines, they should still be absolutely fine to enjoy the next day, especially if closed with a proper stopper, and as champagne has a greater atmospheric pressure than prosecco, it stands to reason that it stays fizzier longer – for up to two days – while prosecco is best enjoyed the day after.

> **DID YOU KNOW?** A spoon, silver or otherwise, placed in a bottle of sparkling wine does not preserve the fizz – it stays sparkling for a day or two anyway!

White wines with high acidity – a dry Riesling or Chablis, for example – can last for a good week or two in the fridge, if not longer, and still be enjoyable. Rounder, riper whites are best consumed within two to three days, and the same goes for reds. Some opened but unfinished reds can actually taste better the next day, but some seem to deteriorate immediately (I find Rioja to be one of those) and it's pretty much impossible just from looking at the bottle to tell which ones improve and which don't.

If you don't end up finishing a bottle and the next day it doesn't taste as good, put it to one side and use it to cook with. Do be aware, however that the life cycle of wine means that all bottles – however expensive and iconic – end up as vinegar, so don't leave it on the side for too long. I once nearly ruined a risotto by using very tired wine, so quickly taste the wine first, before using, to check it's still okay.

> **TIP** Put unfinished reds as well as whites in the fridge – this should give you an extra few days – and remember to remove the bottle twenty minutes before you wish to drink it.

Different Bottle Sizes

Some bottle sizes have different names according to whether they are for still or sparkling wines – the still (Bordeaux typically) names are shown first in each case:

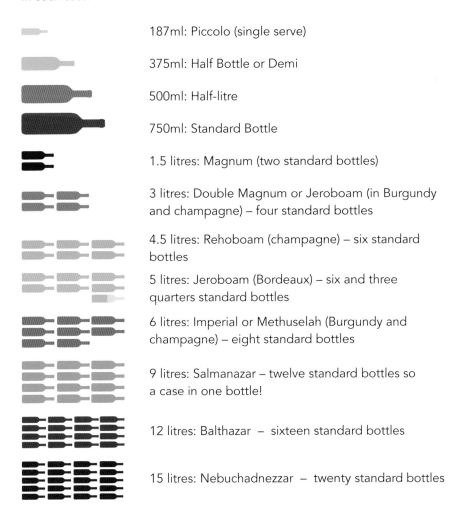

187ml: Piccolo (single serve)

375ml: Half Bottle or Demi

500ml: Half-litre

750ml: Standard Bottle

1.5 litres: Magnum (two standard bottles)

3 litres: Double Magnum or Jeroboam (in Burgundy and champagne) – four standard bottles

4.5 litres: Rehoboam (champagne) – six standard bottles

5 litres: Jeroboam (Bordeaux) – six and three quarters standard bottles

6 litres: Imperial or Methuselah (Burgundy and champagne) – eight standard bottles

9 litres: Salmanazar – twelve standard bottles so a case in one bottle!

12 litres: Balthazar – sixteen standard bottles

15 litres: Nebuchadnezzar – twenty standard bottles

FOOD AND WINE PAIRING 101

If you're looking to pair your food and wine, you'll probably decide what you want to eat first and then select a wine to go with that dish. The food that you want to eat inevitably changes during the year, in line with the weather and seasonal availability – each new season heralds the arrival of different seasonal produce. Generally speaking, when it's hot you want simpler foods – lighter dishes that provide refreshment – and the same applies to your wine choice too – you are likely to fancy something zesty and refreshing. When it's cold however, you're likely to feel partial to warming food and robust reds. Whatever the time of year, though, matching food and wine can sometimes be intimidating, especially if you are preparing for a dinner party or trying to impress.

But if you follow these three simple steps it becomes a whole lot easier.

1. **Match the weight of the wine to the weight of the food:** For me this is key. If you have a delicate seafood dish that is light in both structure and flavour, it makes total sense to marry it with a light, subtle wine – a chunky red would overwhelm the flavours and dominate the dish completely. Conversely, if you are planning on enjoying a robust rib of beef or a richly flavoured, slow-cooked casserole, a full-bodied red will match the weight of the dish really well, whereas a subtly flavoured white would be lost.

2. **What grows together goes together:** Cuisines and ingredients tend to marry brilliantly with their local wines. Spanish reds are fantastic with paella and tapas, while the peachy, minerally Albariño from the coastal Rías Baixas region of north-west Spain is sensational with seafood. Chianti is a sure-fire hit with tomato-based pizza and pasta dishes and English sparkling wines are fabulous with fish and chips. The list really does go on and on.

3. **Flavour balancing:** There may be a whole raft of different flavours or components in a dish, but usually there is one that dominates, and that is the flavour to work with. Suppose you are having chicken. Is it a roast chicken, a chicken curry or a chicken salad? If it's a curry, it isn't the chicken you need to match the wine to, it's the stronger sauce. Is it a korma, a jalfrezi or tandoori? Is it spicy or does it have a coconut or tomato base? You need to consider the main elements of both the food and the wine as ideally you want them to be balanced so there isn't one part that will overwhelm or dominate the other. You also need to consider seasoning; salt enhances the flavour of a dish but it also inhibits the body's ability to detect acidity in wine. As a result it can make wine seem softer and more approachable, making acidic wines taste better with food than on their own. It's important to note though that too much salt can make a wine taste 'flat'; the acidity will be perceived as being too low.

Beyond these three primary rules, another factor to take into consideration when pairing food and wine is how the food you are making is cooked, as that will affect both its texture and taste. Is it raw, roasted, steamed, fried or grilled? Raw foods such as salads and steamed dishes usually pair best with delicate, elegant wines, while more robust roasted, grilled or barbecued foods require wines with more flavour and structure. And finally, you need to decide if you are going to go down the complement or contrast route. Imagine you are making a crab risotto. This is a rich yet quite delicately flavoured dish, so a white wine would be a good choice here. Given the creamy nature of the rice, if you were thinking of going down the 'complement' route, a rounded white like a cool-climate Chardonnay from, say, Australia or South Africa would be a logical choice. However, you might prefer a contrasting wine instead, one that acts like a squeeze of lemon to cut through that richness. If so, a crisper white with higher acidity like a Chablis, Garganega or Falanghina would be an excellent match, as would a dry rosé. For a quick cheat-sheet of wine recommendations for your meal, have a look at the Pairing Wine with Every Food chapter on p. 267.

REMEMBER Usually, you want the weight and intensity of the food and wine to match so that they complement each other but sometimes you can achieve that balance by contrasting them. Often both approaches work, and then it is down, as it so often is, to personal preference.

Final Thoughts on Food and Wine: Matching the Seasons

Many dishes are seasonally (and culturally) specific, from asparagus (spring), corn on the cob and strawberries (summer), blackberries and apples, butternut squash and pumpkins (autumn) through to turkey and comforting casseroles (winter). Some dishes obviously bridge the seasons and thus are 'trans-seasonal'; butternut squash soup for example can be eaten and enjoyed outside of autumn into winter and even into a chilly spring! But regardless of when you are eating a food, its best wine match remains the same. Autumnal foods pair best with autumnal wines, as they share a similar weight of structure and have complementary flavours. If however you aren't a fan say of autumnal whites such as Chardonnay and Viognier, then of course try something else, but always consider the weight of the dish and match it to a wine with a similar body first and foremost.

There are also popular 'family favourite' dishes that are frequently eaten all year round, from lasagne to pizza and burgers, and in these cases some micro-adjustments may need to be made to the wine pairing. Lasagne, for example, is always enjoyable with a fruity red, but try the wine chilled if you are having the lasagne for a summer lunch with salad. A burger with a rich blue-cheese sauce might be ideal with a robust, richly fruited Shiraz in the winter but, served al fresco with salads and leaves in the summer, it might pair better with a robust rosé. Wines should be matched not just to the food, but also the mood and occasion, and these change during the course of the year.

Wines should be matched not just to the food, but also the mood and occasion, and these change during the course of the year.

A Wine For Every Season & Occasion

PART 2

SEASONAL WINES

The second part of this book dives into the four seasons – spring, summer, autumn and winter – and looks at the branches of the Wine Flavour Tree that best match each season. The grape varieties found on those branches are then matched with easy-to-cook recipes that highlight the delicious produce available at that time of year.

Bountiful spring boasts the Green Fruits & Grass branch of the Tree for whites (Sauvignon Blanc, Verdejo, Bacchus, Vermentino) and Currants & Herbs for reds (Cabernet Sauvignon, Touriga Nacional, Carménère, Negroamaro). These wines marry well with such seasonal fare as asparagus, herbs, spring greens and lamb.

Sunny summer introduces two white branches – Orchard Fruits (unoaked Chardonnay, Pinot Grigio, Chenin Blanc, Garganega) and Citrus Fruits (dry Riesling, Sémillon, Grüner Veltliner, Falanghina), great for the lighter meals typically enjoyed al fresco – and reds that suit chilling, which are found on the Soft & Juicy branch (Gamay, Dolcetto, Cinsault and Tarrango). Recipes showcase tomatoes, green beans, salads and sweetcorn.

Cosy autumn is all about comfort, and the wines on both the Stone Fruits branch (Chardonnay, Viognier, Albariño, Fiano) and the Berries & Chocolate branch (Merlot, Tempranillo, Barbera, Nero d'Avola) are smooth and medium-bodied. Enjoy them with risottos, butternut squash soup, mushrooms and chilli con carne.

Chilly winter bears two red fruit branches: Blackberries & Spice (Syrah, Malbec, Zinfandel, Pinotage) and Red Fruits & Roses (Pinot Noir, Grenache, Nebbiolo, Sangiovese), as well as a white branch that works brilliantly with spicy food – Exotic Fruits & Spice (off-dry Riesling, Gewürztraminer, Torrontés, Muscat). Winter warmers include a curry and mini venison Wellingtons served with Brussels sprouts (obvs!) and parsnip purée.

In each seasonal section you will find a 'spotlight' white and/or red grape variety that has been highlighted and expanded on because of its indisputable international importance. These are sometimes referred to as the 'noble' grape varieties, of which there are six: Chardonnay, Riesling and Sauvignon Blanc for whites and Cabernet Sauvignon, Merlot and Pinot Noir for reds, although nowadays they are more likely to simply be referred to as 'international' varieties. The other grapes detailed within each branch section are then ordered according to their popularity and I've given an indication of affordability – per 75cl bottle – by using the following key:

£ = £5 or less

££ = £5–£10

£££ = £10–£20

££££ = £20–£50

£££££ = £50–£100+

Your new wine know-how will make navigating these wines and the wine aisle so much easier, giving you the confidence to select the best bottle for every season and occasion.

Spring

INTRODUCTION

March heralds the beginning of spring: the days grow lighter and mercifully warmer. Early spring can sometimes feel suspiciously similar to winter however, with April showers and cold snaps, so cosy nights in and the desire to continue to hibernate may still feel like the order of the day. But there is a glimmer of hope as the earth wakes up from its sleep and becomes more fecund. Snowdrops and crocuses start to carpet the earth, alongside nodding daffodils, dazzling tulips and beautiful bluebells, offering a feast for the senses after the barren winter. Green shoots and leaves slowly start unfurling and the promise of life and energy is everywhere as the season progresses.

A new season also welcomes different seasonal foods and spring offers an abundance of pretty much everything green! In some countries wild garlic can be found early in the season, joined later by herbs such as basil and mint and an array of green veggies. Winter's heavier root vegetables remain, but there are other fabulous additions to be unearthed too, such as Jersey potatoes. Salad leaves start to put in an appearance as spring nudges nearer to summer, and when it comes to meat, the season is of course synonymous with lamb, the archetypal Easter meal.

Aside from Easter – the Christian celebration of renewal and rebirth that marks the resurrection of Jesus – spring also sees the religious festival of Passover (one of the three pilgrimage festivals).

A major Jewish holiday, Passover celebrates the liberation of the Jews' ancestors from slavery when they were led out of Egypt by Moses. Traditional dishes for Passover include beef brisket and chicken. Ramadan also takes place in the spring, according to the Islamic calendar (the dates change every year), when Muslims fast during daylight hours for a month, finishing with Eid al Fitr – the Festival of the Breaking of the Fast.

Culturally, spring also brings Mother's Day, which is a great opportunity, if one were needed, for enjoying sparkling wines and delighting in bunches of tulips. This takes place in March in the United Kingdom but falls on the second Sunday in May in a number of other countries, including Australia, Canada, China, Germany, New Zealand and the United States. In early spring, following on from Chinese New Year, China celebrates the Spring Festival, which marks the beginning of a new season, a new year and new life. March sees International Women's Day; England's St George's Day falls on 23 April and in the Southern Hemisphere, where it is celebrated, Halloween is a spring occasion rather than an autumn one.

Glorious spring, full of life and optimism, with longer days and warmer (if wetter) weather, coupled with a cornucopia of fresh seasonal fruit and veg just waiting to be enjoyed with perky, zesty, herbal whites and rich, curranty reds.

WHAT'S HAPPENING
IN THE VINEYARD?

Spring in the vineyard heralds the first signs of green, indicating
that the vine has awakened from its winter hibernation and is
bursting back into life. This is called 'budbreak' or 'budburst' and
takes place in March to April in the Northern Hemisphere and
September to October in the Southern Hemisphere. Budbreak sees
small shoots and leaves develop and these shoots need training –
tying to wires, essentially – so that they won't eventually shade the
berries. However, these tender young shoots are at risk of spring
frosts – a huge concern for grape growers as they can decimate
the vineyard, causing any new plant life to die. This can massively
affect a year's crop and so growers try to mitigate against it as much
as possible. Smudge pots (oil burners) or bougies not only look
extraordinarily beautiful when they are lit up at night, but they are
also a vital tool in the fight against the ravages of nature.

SPRING WINE STYLES

Whites

With an abundance of seasonal herbs and green vegetables, nature provides a plethora of fresh 'green' flavours, and the ideal spring whites will mirror this; they are primarily about green fruit flavours and perky freshness. Whites are zingy with energy and verve, light- to medium-bodied and with flavours that marry well with the seasonal produce: herbal, invigorating, fresh and exuberant. The white branch of the Wine Flavour Tree that is best suited to spring is GREEN FRUITS & GRASS, with flavours of gooseberry, grass, elderflower and herbs.

The four grape varieties on this branch – Sauvignon Blanc, Verdejo, Bacchus and Vermentino – perfectly encapsulate the personality of a spring white.

Spring has two 'spotlight' grapes: Sauvignon Blanc and Cabernet Sauvignon.

SAUVIGNON BLANC

(pronounced: Sew-vin-yon-blonk – there's no 'k' on the end if you're using a French accent, although I don't and tend to shorten to Sauvignon!)

This fabulously distinctive French-born white grape variety is one of the most popular in the world and is now grown in pretty much every winemaking country.

In France, the two largest and most prestigious regions for Sauvignon are the Loire Valley – the villages of Pouilly-Fumé and Sancerre, in particular – and Bordeaux.

All Pouilly-Fumé and white Sancerre are made from Sauvignon (red and rosé Sancerre are from Pinot Noir) and the former tends to be slightly riper and richer with notes of orange and even an umami-mushroom note, whereas Sancerre is more linear and racy with elderflower aromas. Other regions to look out for within the Loire include the larger (and cheaper) Touraine as well as Quincy and Menetou-Salon.

While Bordeaux is revered for its reds, it also produces some excellent dry 'Bordeaux Blanc', which is usually made from a blend of Sauvignon and Sémillon (the blended nature of the wine does mean that the Sauvignon character is less obvious than it is in the wines from the Loire). The very best are from the appellations of Pessac-Léognan and Graves where there is – unusually for Sauvignon Blanc – some oak influence on the wines.

DID YOU KNOW? Another example of oaked Sauvignon Blanc is Fumé Blanc in the United States.

Also found in
Everywhere! But notably New Zealand, South Africa, Australia and Chile.
- **New Zealand:** Look out for bottles from Marlborough in particular (home to some 90 per cent of the country's Sauvignon plantings) but also Nelson, both on the South Island.
- **South Africa:** Premium cool-climate regions (Sauvignon prefers a cool-to-moderate climate rather than a warm one) include Stellenbosch, Elgin and Constantia.
- **Australia:** Excellent Sauvignon Blanc is again made in the cooler climate regions such as the Adelaide Hills in South Australia and Margaret River in Western Australia.
- **Chile:** Casablanca and the Leyda Valley are regions to look for on the label. Cheaper wines can be found from the Central Valley but are less varietally distinct.
- Elsewhere, notable plantings are found in Italy, Spain, Hungary, Canada and the United States – especially the aforementioned Fumé Blanc.

WINE FACT Don't confuse Sauvignon Blanc with Savagnin Blanc (also known as Traminer), as the latter predominantly produces '*vin jaune*' in the Jura region of France.

Flavour profile
The flavour profile of Sauvignon subtly changes according to where in the world it is grown but it should always be pungent, green, grassy and herbaceous with crisp acidity. These green notes are derived from a flavour compound called 'methoxypyrazine' (see p. 109).
- **French Sauvignon** tends to be leaner, tighter and more restrained, with notes of elderflower, herbs and grass. The oaked wines from Bordeaux (Pessac-Léognan and Graves) have a subtle spicy note to them and

the Sémillon in the blend makes them waxier and a bit fuller while still displaying herbal notes.
- **New Zealand** really put themselves on the global wine map for Sauvignon due to their sheer pungency and aromatic intensity! The wines are so distinctive, with a huge number of different flavours ranging from passion fruit to asparagus, gooseberry, tomato leaf and grass.
- **South African Sauvignon** displays distinctive notes of green pepper or capsicum.
- **Australian and Chilean Sauvignon** also taste of green fruits but also green pepper and citrus such as grapefruit and lime.

Food and occasions

This grape is terrific with nibbles, charcuterie and green vegetables such as asparagus, but it also works well with goat's cheese (a simple goat's cheese salad, for example), tomatoes and herby fish cakes or, indeed, anything with a herb-based sauce, whether that be with chives, dill, tarragon, parsley or basil – enjoy with pesto. The more delicate wines (think Sancerre) complement delicate flavours, so seafood (prawns especially) or goat's cheese (again) are top choices. For unoaked examples that are riper and a bit more tropical, try a savoury veg-packed tart, stuffed peppers, simple steamed asparagus with Parmesan shavings or trout and pea purée. For wines with a bit of oak you can dial up the flavour and texture of the food, so a juicy roast chicken or salmon en croûte would work well. Ideal for a Mother's Day treat.

Affordability £–£££

There is a huge amount of Sauvignon Blanc on the market and consequently it remains extremely good value. Though you'd have to pay more for a Sancerre or a high-end bottle from Bordeaux, there are still a lot of cheaper mass-market brands available.

BACCHUS
(pronounced: Back-uh-s)

Bacchus was created in 1933 by crossing different grape varieties and is mainly found in the German regions of Franken, Pfalz, Nahe and Rheinhessen.

Also found in
Bacchus thrives in the United Kingdom and is the second most planted white variety after Chardonnay. Preferring cooler climates, it can also be found (in tiny amounts) in Canada.

Flavour profile
Bacchus displays distinctive notes of elderflower that are extremely similar stylistically to Sauvignon Blanc. It is also light-bodied, herbal scented and typically unoaked, but with lower acidity. It is made for 'early drinking' – to be consumed as close to its production (or vintage) year as possible.

Food and occasion
Drink with seafood, fish and chips, spring veggies, goat's cheese and tomatoes. And why not open a bottle of Bacchus on St George's Day!

Affordability £££
As a result of the relatively small quantities produced, Bacchus is rather expensive.

WINE FACT The Bacchus grape variety shares its name with the Roman god of wine, aka Dionysus in Greek mythology.

If the wines are labelled 'Rueda', then Verdejo has to comprise 50 per cent of the blend and if 'Rueda Verdejo', then 85 per cent minimum. Occasionally Verdejo is oaked and these wines can be utterly delicious!

VERDEJO
(pronounced: Ver-dec-oh)

Verdejo is a delicious Spanish grape variety found in the north-west region of Rueda.

Also found in
Native to Spain.

Flavour profile
Verdejo is light, herbal and grassy – reminiscent of the Sauvignon Blanc with which it is so often blended, but also with hints of lime and fennel. The oaked styles have notes of spice while Verdejo that has been aged in bottle displays aromas of almonds.

Food and occasion
Goat's cheese, tomatoes, gazpacho, red peppers, fried fish, salads and seafood; think *gambas al ajillo*. This wine is ideal for those warmer late spring days that can take you entirely by surprise, making you rush to sit outside and eat al fresco with friends and family.

Affordability ££–£££
Not the cheapest because it pretty much comes exclusively from one region in Spain. The unoaked bottles cost less than the oaked ones.

DID YOU KNOW? Verdejo and the similarly sounding Portuguese Verdelho grape from Madeira are NOT the same!

VERMENTINO
(pronounced: Ver-men-tea-no)

An Italian variety; on the island of Sardinia it is the most planted white grape variety, with the best region being Vermentino di Gallura DOCG to the north-east of the island.

Also found in
Predominantly France (including Corsica), where it goes by the name of Rolle and can be found in many Provençal blends, both white and, especially, rosé. There are now more plantings in France than in Italy. Australia is also making Vermentino.

Flavour profile
Like the other whites on the Green Fruits & Grass branch of the Tree, the wines are usually unoaked, fresh and light-bodied with crisp acidity. There are notes of herbs, grass, orange and apricot, as well as hints of lime and almond: so very similar to Verdejo.

Food and occasion
This zippy wine loves Mediterranean dishes like spaghetti alle vongole, fregola (a bit like couscous) with seafood, saffron risotto (not dissimilar to paella) or salmon with a pesto crust. It's equally delicious with spring veggies and lighter dishes sprinkled with herbs. It would make a great choice next time you're in an Italian restaurant or re-creating the *trattoria* vibe at home.

Affordability ££–£££
Vermentino is generally mid-range. It's not always the easiest to find but should be available on most shelves and at a decent price as you aren't paying for any time in barrel because the wines are typically unoaked.

SPRING WINE STYLES

Reds

Spring whites are united by being light-bodied, energetic and fresh, with distinctive 'green' notes, and spring reds also display these 'green' flavours, the result of the aforementioned flavour compound 'methoxypyrazine'. Present in Sauvignon Blanc, it is also found in varieties such as Cabernet Sauvignon and Carménère, and is responsible for the flavours of herbs, blackcurrant leaf and green pepper found in these wines. It will come as no surprise, therefore, that the branch of the Tree that boasts great reds for spring drinking is CURRANTS & HERBS.

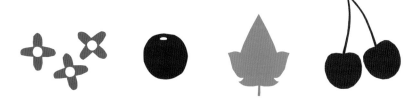

The four red grape varieties that feature on this branch are Cabernet Sauvignon, Touriga Nacional, Carménère and Negroamaro. Cabernet Sauvignon and Carménère both have lots of these wonderful cassis leaf notes and the green, minty flavours complement the new season's spring lamb brilliantly, making these reds ideal for Easter celebrations. Wines made from all four of these red grapes tend to be quite structured and are medium- to full-bodied: ideal for red meat and those colder, wetter spring days!

CABERNET SAUVIGNON
(pronounced: Cab-er-nay sew-vin-yon)

Like its mother, Sauvignon Blanc (Cabernet Sauvignon's parents are
Sauvignon Blanc and Cabernet Franc), it is distinctive, flavoursome
and has also proved to be extremely adept at being transported
around the world.

Unsurprisingly, due to its parentage, Cabernet Sauvignon is a French grape
variety and is most famously found in the Bordeaux region – named after
the local city of the same name. The other red grape varieties that are
widely grown in Bordeaux and are often blended with the late-ripening
Cabernet Sauvignon include Merlot, Cabernet Franc and Petit Verdot.
Merlot is an early-ripening grape and also softer and fruitier, so adds a bit
of charm and approachability to the leaner tannic structure of Cabernet,
whereas Cabernet Franc adds a green, cassis leaf note along with a
distinct pencil lead lift (which is nicer than it sounds!). Petit Verdot is deeply
coloured and slightly spicy and acts like a touch of seasoning to the blends.

Whether Cabernet Sauvignon is the majority component in a blend
depends on which side of the Gironde Estuary a red wine is from. It is in
the vineyards situated on the Left Bank, with their famous gravel soils, that
Cabernet really flourishes, in appellations such as the Médoc and Haut-
Médoc (both north of the city of Bordeaux) and Graves (to the south). Within
the Haut-Médoc are the fine wine regions of St-Estèphe, Pauillac, St-Julien
and Margaux.

DID YOU KNOW? Claret is another word for red Bordeaux, with most
claret being generic Bordeaux AOC.

The so-called 1855 classification (which, as the name suggests, was drawn up in that year) created the 'classed growths' of the Médoc and Graves. The region's best wines were essentially graded and qualitatively placed in one of the five different growths:

- **The First Growths:** Château Haut-Brion, Château Lafite-Rothschild, Château Latour, Château Margaux and Château Mouton Rothschild. These are regarded as five of the very best (and most expensive) wines in the world.
- **The Second Growths:** There are fourteen in total and the 'Super Seconds' include big hitters such as Château Cos d'Estournel, Château Ducru-Beaucaillou and Château Pichon-Longueville Comtesse de Lalande.
- **The Third (fourteen), Fourth (ten) and Fifth Growths (eighteen châteaux):** Illustrious names such as Château Palmer, Château Beychevelle and Château Lynch Bages. They are still expensive but not as pricey as the First Growths.

It is worth bearing in mind that the 'big name' growths produced here make up only a fraction of the region's wines, with generic Bordeaux AOC being the largest appellation. For other better-value wines also look for Crus Bourgeois on the label or for wines from Moulis and Listrac.

Also found in

- **Italy:** Renowned for the iconic Super Tuscan wines which use Cabernet in the blends.
- **California:** World-class Cabernet Sauvignon is found here – specifically in Napa. They are varietally distinctive but with polished fruit and supple tannins.
- **Australia:** Makes fantastic single varietal wines, as the warmer climate largely mitigates against the need to blend. Look for South Australia on the label and Coonawarra in particular – Cabernet loves the distinctive, red 'terra rossa' soils found there – and Margaret River in Western Australia.
- **New Zealand:** Cabernet tends to comprise part of a blend, and in Hawke's Bay (especially Gimblett Gravels) the highly acclaimed reds tend to be Bordeaux-style blends.

Wherever Cabernet is grown, it has the same deep, rich and almost inky colour. The combination of small berries and thick skins means that the skins can impart a lot of flavour and structure (tannins) to the more limited flesh of the grape. Colour (anthocyanins) and tannins (polyphenols) are both found in these skins and are imparted through careful management during the winemaking process.

- **South Africa:** although it has its very own red grape variety in the form of Pinotage, Cabernet Sauvignon is the country's most planted red variety with many of the best wines coming from Stellenbosch.
- **Others:** Chile has Carménère and Argentina has Malbec, but they also produce world-class Cabernet wines; regions to look out for include the Colchagua and Maipo valleys in Chile and Mendoza in Argentina.

Flavour profile

Aromas and flavours of blackcurrant (cassis), black cherry, mint (can be quite like eucalyptus in Australia), cedar, blackcurrant leaf, tobacco, green pepper and, if there was any oak ageing, spice.

Food and occasions

The combination of Cabernet Sauvignon and red meat is a bit of a no-brainer as the fat in meat helps to tame those tight tannins, which softens the wine. Lamb, in particular, is a great choice as the minty flavours act a bit like mint sauce. So if you're celebrating Easter and eating lamb, a blackcurranty, minty Cabernet should absolutely be your first choice. Roast lamb, lamb chops, shepherd's pie and lamb shanks – they all work, as would beef (from steak to a juicy burger) or chargrilled vegetables.

Affordability £–£££££

Cabernet Sauvignon runs the gamut of affordability, with the cheapest wines tending to come from the Central Valley in Chile, but to really appreciate the depth, intensity and varietal purity of the world's favourite red, trade up a fraction if you can.

TOURIGA NACIONAL

(pronounced: Toor-ee-ga nach-on-al)

Touriga Nacional is a Portuguese grape variety that comprises part of the famous port blends as well as still red wines. It is grown primarily in the Douro (where port is from) and also in the Dāo region.

Also found in
There are some plantings in Spain, the United States and, increasingly, Australia.

Flavour profile
Aromas of violets and rich dark fruits such as black cherry, blackcurrant, blueberry and blackberry. Spicy notes will be evident in wines that have been oaked.

Food and occasions
A superb partner for lamb cooked any way you like – from a roast, to shanks, casseroles, hot pots or pies – but Touriga Nacional also works well with sausages, meatloaf, burgers, mushroom stroganoff or a cauliflower steak. This is a wine for the kind of spring day when it's wet and windy outside and the temptation to hide away with a warming red gets too much!

Affordability ££–£££
Portugal is a treasure trove of good value, well-made wines crafted from indigenous grape varieties – Touriga Nacional is a real favourite of mine.

CARMÉNÈRE
(pronounced Car-mehn-err)

Carménère is a French grape variety that used to be widely grown in Bordeaux. Today it flourishes in its new South American home of Chile, especially in the Colchagua, Rapel and Maipo valleys.

Also found in
Although Italy also has some notable plantings, an impressive 98 per cent of the world's plantings of Carménère are found in Chile.

Flavour profile
Aromas of green pepper, mint, herbs and blackcurrant leaf, as well as blackcurrant, black cherries and dark mint chocolate. The wines are medium- to full-bodied and tend to be deeply coloured and well structured.

Food and occasions
Simple pork, lamb and beef dishes are all delicious with Carménère, but to really make it shine and enhance those herbal notes, introduce a South American chimichurri sauce. Pesto, roasted vegetables (especially peppers) or even a mild tomato-based curry work well with it too. It's another classic spring wine, this time working as a reviving red after an afternoon at the allotment.

Affordability ££
Chile has a reputation for providing purse-friendly wine, and Carménère is no exception. The deeper, richer and more complex bottles will cost more.

WINE FACT Carménère was incorrectly identified as Merlot for many years.

NEGROAMARO

(pronounced: Neh-gro-ah-mah-row)

Negroamaro – meaning 'dark' and 'bitter' – is a southern Italian grape variety widely grown in the warm Mediterranean regions of Puglia and Salento. Aside from producing characterful red wines, it can also make delicious rosé.

Also found in
Native to Italy.

Flavour profile
Deep in colour, full-bodied and quite chunky, with fairly high levels of alcohol, Negroamaro has flavours of black fruits – especially black cherry, but also plums and blackberries – and a suggestion of herbs as well as prominent, though not bitter, tannins.

Food and occasions
The robust Negroamaro can cope with bold, assertive flavours, so be inspired by dishes found in warm Mediterranean climates. Think spaghetti puttanesca, aubergine caponata, meatballs, butterflied lamb, antipasti such as salami, moussaka, barbecued pulled pork, pizza and also hard cheeses such as Parmesan. Transport yourself to foreign climes with an 'Italian evening' at home or order a bottle next time you are at your favourite *pizzeria*.

Affordability ££–£££
A reliable mid-priced bottle of wine with lots of flavour and fruit for the price, courtesy of all that sunshine.

CABERNET FRANC
(pronounced: Cab-er-nay fron)

Another French grape variety that is grown in Bordeaux and the Loire Valley, in appellations such as Chinon, St-Nicolas-de-Bourgueil and Saumur-Champigny.

Also found in
This grape can also be found in the south-west of France, in Bergerac and Madiran, and there are some fabulous examples in Italy (Friuli-Venezia Giulia and Tuscany), Chile and the United States.

Flavour profile
The wines tend to have an appealing fragrance of pencil lead and blackcurrant leaf, along with mint, herbs and some plum, cherry and berry fruits too.

Food and occasions
Light enough to pair with chicken (try it with wild garlic butter), meatier fish like tuna and also rustic fare such as pâté, hams, bread and so on. This is the wine to pack with your picnic on a sunny spring day – the fresher styles can even be served chilled if it's warm!

Affordability ££–£££
Not the cheapest grape to buy but rather mid-range to mid-range plus.

REMEMBER Along with Sauvignon Blanc, Cabernet Franc is the other parent of Cabernet Sauvignon.

SPRING FOOD AND WINE MATCHING

After the carb fest of winter, spring's lighter, fresher produce is just what we need as we shed our jumpers and look to embrace less stodgy food that also happens to be healthy, delicious and easy to prepare. To complement spring's green and vibrant flavours look no further than the Green Fruits & Grass branch of the Wine Flavour Tree; here are grape varieties that are also light, zippy and refreshing, mirroring the notes of the food. The red wines on the Currants & Herbs branch share the same green notes but they are robust enough to pair with lamb, roasted Mediterranean vegetables or herb-packed sauces such as pesto, salsa verde or chimichurri.

Try to follow basic food and wine matching principles; so perky and/or elegant whites cry out for vegetables – such as the delicate asparagus and lemon tagliatelle – but also fish (the trout with crushed peas looks and tastes really impressive but is super simple to make). A riper, fleshier white is required for chicken, which marries with one of my all-time favourites: a lightly oaked white Bordeaux, with the spicy notes from the oak ageing adding texture.

For red wines – and at the risk or repeating myself – lamb is absolutely the 'go-to' meat for every single spring variety on the Currants & Herbs branch, but if (like me) you don't eat lamb then swap it for red peppers stuffed with tomatoes, olives, lentils, feta and herbs (a drizzle of Greek yogurt optional).

What's in season in the spring?

HERBS
basil, chervil, chives, coriander, dill, mint, oregano, parsley, rosemary, sage, sorrel, tarragon, thyme

SALADS
lettuce, rocket, watercress

GREEN VEGGIES
asparagus, broccoli, kale, leeks, peas, purple sprouting broccoli, spinach, spring greens

OTHER VEGGIES
carrots, cauliflower, Jersey royal potatoes, new potatoes, onions, radishes, samphire, spring onions, swede, wild garlic

FRUIT
apricot, elderflower, rhubarb, strawberries

FISH AND SEAFOOD
bream, clams, cockles, cuttlefish, dover sole, gurnard, haddock, plaice, mackerel, monkfish, mussels, oysters, red mullet, seabass, squid, turbot, whitebait

MEAT
beef, chicken, hare, lamb, pork venison, wild boar

FOOD TYPE	BEST WINE TYPES: Green Fruits & Grass and Currants & Herbs
Herbs:	Cabernet Sauvignon, Carménère, Sauvignon Blanc, Verdejo, Vermentino
Salads:	Sauvignon Blanc, Verdejo
Green veggies:	Bacchus, Cabernet Sauvignon, Carménère, Sauvignon Blanc, Vermentino
Other veggies:	Cabernet Franc, Cabernet Sauvignon, Negroamaro, Touriga Nacional
Fish and seafood:	Bacchus, Cabernet Franc, Sauvignon Blanc, Verdejo, Vermentino
Meat (inc. poultry):	Cabernet Franc, Cabernet Sauvignon, Negroamaro, Sauvignon Blanc, Touriga Nacional, Vermentino

SPRING RECIPES

Tagliatelle with Asparagus and Lemon – 122

—

Trout Fillets with Crushed Peas – 123

—

Roast Chicken with Thyme served with Spring
Greens and Purple Sprouting Broccoli – 124

—

Lamb Steaks with Spring Salsa Verde – 125

TAGLIATELLE WITH ASPARAGUS AND LEMON

I cooked this for my twin sister when she was staying once and we had it twice in one week because we both liked it so much. It is fresh, vibrant, extremely simple and – an added bonus – it's also pretty cheap!

+ WINE The zesty nature of this dish calls out for a crisp white and using the adage of 'what grows together goes together', I'd suggest an Italian white – one made from the Vermentino grape, for example. Having said that, anything from this branch of the Wine Flavour Tree would work well with the green notes of the asparagus and the zesty lemon flavours, so you could also try a Spanish Verdejo from Rueda.

SERVES 4

2x tbsp olive oil
2x 200g pack of asparagus
2x cloves garlic, peeled and sliced
1x 500gm bag of fresh egg pasta tagliatelle
1x lemon, zest and juice
Knob of butter
Plenty of Parmesan
Seasoning – salt and a good grind of pepper

Heat a saucepan of salted water for the pasta and also some water at the bottom of a steamer for the asparagus. Gently heat the olive oil in a large frying pan ready for the sliced garlic.

Prepare the asparagus – snap off the woody ends and cut the remaining spears into inch-long pieces and steam for 2–4 minutes depending on the width of the spears until cooked but with some bite, then set aside.

While the asparagus is steaming, fry the garlic in the warmed oil for a few minutes, taking care it doesn't burn. Put the pasta in the boiling water for 3–4 minutes and now zest and juice the lemons.

Once the garlic has softened add the asparagus along with the lemon zest, juice, a knob of butter, a further teaspoon of olive oil and a sprinkling of salt. Taste and add more zest and juice if required, though it should be spot on.

When the pasta is ready, strain and add it to the frying pan and mix with the asparagus and lemon. Serve, sprinkled with Parmesan and plenty of black pepper.

TROUT FILLETS WITH CRUSHED PEAS

A delicate yet satisfying spring dish that feels sophisticated but is deceptively easy to make, marrying soft, subtly flavoured fish with a pop of seasonal mashed green peas. If you're hungry or craving a carbohydrate then serve with some baby potatoes and a knob of butter.

+ WINE You don't want to overwhelm the delicate flavours of this dish, so a lighter French Sauvignon Blanc such as a Sancerre or Quincy would be delicious. Alternatively, a zesty elderflower-scented Bacchus would be exceptional with the lemon thyme notes.

SERVES 4

4x trout fillets
Salt and pepper
500g podded or
    frozen peas
1x level tbsp chopped
    fresh lemon thyme

Vinaigrette:
1x tbsp lemon juice
1x tbsp sherry vinegar
5x tbsp olive oil
Salt and pepper

Preheat the oven to 200/180°C fan.

Season the trout with salt and pepper and roast in the oven (skin side down) until cooked but still moist – about 10 minutes.

While the fish is cooking, make the pea mash and the vinaigrette. Simply boil the peas in water (my preferences is fresh rather than frozen peas) for around 4 minutes until soft, strain, return to the saucepan and crush with a fork until nicely broken down.

Combine all of the vinaigrette ingredients in a small bowl or jug and add to the peas along with the lemon thyme. Mix well.

Plate up the pea mash and top with a trout fillet along with a sprinkle of lemon thyme leaves if you are feeling fancy!

SPRING

ROAST CHICKEN WITH THYME SERVED WITH SPRING GREENS AND PURPLE SPROUTING BROCCOLI

A roast chicken is so versatile – enjoy it for lunch on Sunday with all the trimmings or pop it in the oven and serve with a salad for a mid-week supper. An added bonus is that the left-over carcass can be used to make a fantastic stock for soups or risotto. This dish is delicious on any day of the week and with spring's favourite starch – buttered new potatoes.

+ **WINE** Taking into account the weight of the white meat and the citrus and herb flavours, a ripe, textured, flavourful Southern Hemisphere Sauvignon – from New Zealand or South Africa – would be terrific. Alternatively, a lightly oaked white Sauvignon blend from Bordeaux would be tasty with the roast 'chook'.

SERVES 4

1x 1.5kg chicken
A glug of olive oil, around 2 tbsp
2x sprigs fresh thyme, leaves picked
Seasoning – salt and pepper
Half a lemon

For the spring greens:
200g purple sprouting broccoli, trimmed
200g spring greens
1x tbsp olive oil
1x small clove garlic, crushed
Zest and juice of half a lemon

Preheat the oven to 220/200°C fan.

Put the chicken in a roasting tin and then glug over the olive oil before scattering the thyme leaves on top along with a twist of pepper and a sprinkling of salt. Insert the lemon half into the cavity. Roast for 20 minutes at 220/200°C fan before reducing the temperature to 200/180°C fan for a further 45 minutes, making sure that the chicken is cooked through: the juices will run clear when cooked. Remove from the oven, cover with foil and allow to rest for a further 10 minutes.

Meanwhile, trim the veggies and steam until tender – around 5 minutes, checking the thickest parts of the stems with a sharp knife to see if they are done. To make the dressing, combine the olive oil, garlic, lemon zest and juice in a small bowl or jug. Pour over the vegetables when they are ready. Serve immediately with the chicken.

LAMB STEAKS WITH SPRING SALSA VERDE

Traditional Easter lamb is transformed by the addition of a punchy salsa verde. I could literally spoon it straight into my mouth, it's so good! I always serve this with buttery baby carrots and waxy new potatoes.

+ **WINE** The robust flavours in this dish should be partnered with an equally punchy red, ideally one with notes of mint and herbs to enhance the herbal notes of the salsa verde. Any red from the Currants & Herbs branch would be a winner, but my top choices would be a mint-laden, cool-climate Coonawarra Cabernet from Australia or a blackcurrant-leaf-flavoured Chilean Carménère.

SERVES 4

4x lamb leg steaks

For the marinade:
Half a head of garlic with each clove peeled and halved
4x tbsp olive oil
2x sprigs of rosemary
20x whole black peppercorns

For the salsa verde:
1x clove of garlic, crushed
1x handful of fresh mint, chopped
1x handful of flat leaf parsley, chopped
15x basil leaves, chopped
1x tbsp small capers, drained and chopped
Zest of 1 lemon
A small handful of gherkins, finely chopped
2x anchovy fillets, chopped
2x tsp Dijon mustard
2x tbsp red wine vinegar
3x tbsp olive oil
A good grind of black pepper

Combine all of the marinade ingredients in a sealable food bag with the lamb steaks and then transfer to the fridge to marinate for a few hours or overnight if time.

Heat a griddle or frying pan on a medium-plus heat (you don't need any oil) and then cook the steaks for 2 to 3 minutes on each side, depending on how pink you like your meat and how thick the steaks are. Remove from the pan, put on a plate, cover with foil and rest for about 10 minutes.

While the lamb is resting make the salsa verde – simply prepare and then combine all of the ingredients in a small bowl – it couldn't be easier!

SPRING

OTHER SPRING WINE STYLES

Sparkling Wines

With their perky acidity, refreshing mousse (bubbles) and general air of optimism, sparkling wines are the ultimate vinous mood enhancer. Like a glorious spring day, they are almost guaranteed to put a 'spring' in your step, coupled with the fact that the carbon dioxide in the wines gets the alcohol into your bloodstream faster, resulting in what I call a 'fizzy lift'!

DID YOU KNOW? To make any sparkling wine, you have to start with a base still wine (called *vin clair* in Champagne) to which **sugar** and **yeast** are added. This causes the wine to ferment again, and as ever, a by-product of this (second) fermentation is carbon dioxide. In still wine production you want this CO_2 to escape, but for sparkling wines you need to trap it as it dissolves into the wine, creating that all important mousse.

Sparkling wines can be made in one of six different ways, but the two methods most commonly used (by far) are:

- **Tank method (also called Charmat or cuve close):** when the second fermentation takes place in a tank
- **Traditional method:** when the second fermentation takes place in the actual bottle you buy

The other four ways to make sparkling wine are:

- **Transfer method:** when the wine is fermented in a bottle, as per the traditional method, but is then transferred into a tank for the clarification (cleaning) and finishing of the wine. It is then re-bottled and sold in a different bottle to the one it was fermented in. This is often used in Australia, New Zealand, the United States and for atypical bottle formats (e.g. large bottles). The **transversage method** is almost identical but clarification occurs before the transfer.
- **Ancestral method:** how 'Pét-Nat' or *pétillant naturel* is made. The wine undergoes only one fermentation and is bottled whilst it is taking place resulting in a very gentle mousse.
- **Carbonation:** used for aromatic styles such as sparkling New Zealand Sauvignon Blanc.
- **Continuous method:** or Russian method, which passes the wine through a series of tanks.

Tank method sparkling wines

The most popular tank method sparkling wine is undoubtedly prosecco and the way that it is made accounts for its pale colour, larger bubbles (compared to champagne) and fruity nature. Prosecco is produced in north-east Italy, in the Veneto and Friuli regions and from the Glera grape, with pink prosecco having some Pinot Nero (Pinot Noir) in the blend. The grape itself used to be called Prosecco but was changed to Glera in 2009 to prevent other countries from being able to make prosecco! Happily, there happened to be a village by the name of Prosecco in Friuli and so now no producers from outside the designated zone can give their wines that name. Prosecco is quality level DOC but there are two DOCG areas that produce superior wines called Conegliano-Valdobbiadene (or Con-Val) and Asolo.

More serious styles of prosecco, called *Col Fondo*, are also made and are quite delicious, if somewhat different from the usual style. Rather than being tank fermented, they are bottle fermented and closed under a crown cap rather than cork. They can be a bit cloudy from the sediment that is left in the bottle and are also dry, with a dried fruit character. These are 'natural' wines and this style of winemaking is called 'pét-nat' or 'methode ancestrale'.

Lambrusco – another sparkling Italian wine, but red – is also made using the tank method, as is Asti and the cheaper German Sekt (the better bottles use the traditional or transfer method).

Traditional method sparkling wines

Champagne

The Champagne region, to the north of Paris, has a cold climate and historically the wines made there were still. A happy accident, however, led to the discovery of sparkling wines that were, in fact, really rather good. Over the years this has been attributed to none other than the famous winemaking monk Dom Pérignon, who is believed to have said, 'Come quickly, I am tasting the stars!' What is likely to have happened is that as the weather warmed up, the dormant (but not dead) yeasts in the wine awoke from their slumber, had an available nutrient source by way of some residual sugar and made the wine re-ferment, transforming it into sparkling wine. Though the Dom Pérignon story is certainly a fabulous one, it was actually an Englishman, Sir Christopher Merret (also spelt Merrett) who detailed secondary fermentation about six years before the famous Frenchman was attributed with the making of champagne as we know it today.

There are three main grape varieties in the Champagne region: Chardonnay, Pinot Noir and Pinot Meunier (just Meunier in France). Interestingly, Chardonnay is the only white of the three, and yet, despite typically being made predominantly from red grapes – a classic blend has one third of each variety – champagne is, of course, white (unless it's rosé!) The reason for this is that a wine grape's juice is pretty much colourless; it is the skins of the berries that are responsible for the magic of colour, structure and flavour in wine. Once the ripe grapes are picked (by hand), the whole bunches are pressed extremely gently so that no colour or bitterness ends up in the wine.

When a champagne is made from white grapes only it is called **Blanc de Blancs** and when it is made from the red grapes only, **Blanc de Noirs**. Chardonnay adds elegance and a certain verve and tautness to the blend. Pinot Noir brings mid-palate weight and structure, whereas Pinot Meunier provides more of an upfront fruitiness.

For rosé champagne, colour is usually achieved simply by adding red wine – usually Pinot Noir – during the blending process of the still base *vin clair*, until the desired hue is achieved.

Vintage champagne uses a base wine that comes exclusively from the named vintage on the label, whereas for non-vintage champagne the blend is created both from that year's wine and also from 'reserve' wines, which are a blend of different, older vintages. This allows for the creation of a consistent 'house' style, which is especially important for 'les grandes maisons (or *grande marque*) de Champagne' – the famous household names, such as Bollinger or Moët & Chandon – who want each and every bottle of their non-vintage wines to reflect their signature style.

Once the base still wine has been blended – taking into account different grape varieties, vineyard sites and even vintages with the use of reserve wines – it is ready for the addition of a solution called the *liqueur de tirage* (made up predominantly of wine, sugar and specific champagne yeasts), which kicks off that all-important second fermentation. The wine is then transferred into bottles and closed with a crown cap. And then the magic of champagne happens . . .

Once the yeasts have used up their nutrient source (the sugar), they die and it is the contact of the dead yeast cells with the liquid – called **yeast autolysis** – that creates all those wonderful bready, bakery, nutty notes that champagne is known for. Non-vintage champagne legally has to spend a minimum of twelve months on those dead yeast cells and vintage champagne three years.

DID YOU KNOW? 'Grower champagne' is made by smaller, independent growers who not only own the vineyard but also make their wines. Most will also sell grapes to the big houses.

The last part of the production of champagne is to remove the dead yeast from the bottle. This used to be done by hand, whereby the bottles were turned in the dark cellars to slowly move the yeast into the neck of the bottle – a process called 'riddling' – but this is now typically performed by mechanical gyropalattes. Once the yeast plug is removed (disgorging), the *liqueur d'expedition* or dosage is added – a mix of cane sugar dissolved in wine – to 'top up' the wine and adjust the final sweetness.

> **DID YOU KNOW?** In Champagne, some wines, whether they are *grande marque* or grower champagne, might have **Premier Cru** or **Grand Cru** on the label. If this is the case, then 100 per cent of the grapes that have gone into that bottle will be superior fruit from one of the seventeen Grand Cru or forty-two Premier Cru villages.

Crémant

Crémant are French, traditional method sparkling wines made outside of the Champagne region. There are eight AOCs – such as Crémant de Loire and Crémant de Bordeaux – all of which are made from different permitted grape varieties.

Cava

Spanish cava (meaning cellar) is predominantly produced in the Catalonia region and is also made by the traditional method, typically using indigenous grapes such as Macabeo (otherwise known as Viura), Parellada and Xarel-Lo, though a handful of others are permitted. While non-vintage champagne must spend twelve months on the lees, cava need only spend nine months.

English sparkling wine

England makes excellent – though not exclusively – traditional method sparkling wines in the same vein as champagne, having the same chalky soils and grape varieties. The climate is cooler than in France, however, so English sparkling wines tend to have more elevated levels of citrus acidity. The majority of vineyards are found in the warmer south of the country in counties such as Surrey, Sussex and Cornwall with Essex being renowned for producing superlative grapes, especially in the Crouch Valley.

Cap Classique

These South African sparklers are generally made from a blend of Chardonnay and Pinot Noir which must, like cava, spend a minimum of nine months on the lees.

Others

Italian Franciacorta is also made in the traditional method and from a blend of Chardonnay and Pinot Noir (or Nero), sometimes with the addition of Pinot Bianco, with eighteen months on lees required for non-vintage wines and thirty for vintage wines. Riservas demand sixty months.

In the Rest of the World, a number of champagne houses have set up wineries in the United States and Australia, with the latter also making distinctive, deeply coloured red, sparkling Shiraz wines – using both the tank and traditional method – which are usually off-dry and sometimes lightly oaked.

In New Zealand, excellent traditional method sparkling wines can be made, but keep an eye out for sparkling Sauvignon Blanc, too: these are primarily carbonated – when CO_2 is pumped into a tank of wine – resulting in wines that are aromatic, flavourful, good value and great fun!

Understanding sweetness in sparkling wines

The sweetness levels of sparkling wines – measured in grams per litre (g/l) of residual sugar or RS – can be found on the labels and, going from dry to sweet, they are as follows:

- **Brut Nature or Zero Dosage:** 0–3g/l RS – very dry and crisp; these styles can be a bit austere
- **Extra Brut:** 0–6g/l RS – still somewhat on the dry side
- **Brut:** 0–12g/l RS – the most popular style/dosage for champagne
- **Extra Dry:** 12–17g/l RS – slightly off-dry, this is the most popular style/dosage for prosecco
- **Dry (Secco):** 17–32g/l RS – this will now be noticeably off-dry
- **Demi-sec:** 32–50g/l – a great choice for a lighter, not too sweet, fruit-based pudding
- **Doux:** 50g/l + – definitely on the sweet side

Summer

INTRODUCTION

The world comes alive in the summer and 'the sounds of the season' are utterly evocative: lawnmowers mowing, ice-cream vans tinkling, children laughing, running in and out of sprinklers, the whack of a tennis or cricket ball, waves lapping on beaches, barbecues sizzling, corks popping and ice cubes clinking! Shoes make way for flip-flops, the nights are long and warm, and life just seems to become more relaxed, with impromptu picnics, al fresco dining and an embarrassment of delicious seasonal produce.

In a way, summer seems to be its own special occasion with a 'sunshine sheen' over the season. It's a time to be outdoors, and many of the season's big cultural events embrace that, from a profusion of music festivals (think Burning Man and Glastonbury), to the Edinburgh Fringe in Scotland, the Pride Parade and

Independence Day celebrations in the United States and the Dragon Boat Festival and Yi Torch Festival in China. The Summer Solstice is celebrated around the world, along with Bastille Day in France, La Tomatina (the tomato throwing festival) in Spain and New Year's Eve fireworks in Sydney, Australia. Religious festivals include the Hajj Pilgrimage in Saudi Arabia and the Krishna Janmashtami in India.

With the warmer weather comes a desire for fuss-free food and salads, as our bodies hanker for lighter produce with a higher water content. Consequently, wine drinking becomes more about refreshment, about fun and uncomplicated drinking; we seek wines that match the upbeat nature of the season – wines that are citrus-scented, juicy and joyful.

WHAT'S HAPPENING IN THE VINEYARD?

Unsurprisingly, this is the season when a lot of growth occurs in the vineyard leading up to autumn's harvest. In the spring, budbreak brought the first signs of growth and those burgeoning shoots had to be trained along various trellising systems for optimal vine health.

Around eight weeks after budbreak, the little buds turn into flowers. For flowering, the vine likes sunlight and dry weather, which are especially important for fruit set, when the flowers transform into fruit that will ultimately become the bunches of grapes. Sometimes – mainly due to bad weather – fruit set is poor and this is known as *coulure*. Obviously if fewer flowers become grapes the eventual yield will be negatively impacted.

The grapes ripen and grow during the summer and *veraison* is when the berries stop growing, finish their ripening and red grapes take on their colour.

SUMMER WINE STYLES

Whites

Summer is undoubtedly the season when white – and of course rosé – wines really come into their own. If spring whites are all about enhancing and elevating the green and herbal notes of that season's produce, then summer whites are predominantly about refreshment, provided by crisp acidity. The warmer weather demands wines that are mouth-watering, while lighter meals – think salads and seafood – mean that subtly scented and flavoured vinos are the order of the day.

Two white branches on the Wine Flavour Tree are primarily associated with summer imbibing. The first, ORCHARD FRUITS, is the lowest branch on the Tree. Consequently, the grape varieties on it tend to make wines that are lighter and fresher, with modest alcohol levels and more restrained aromas and flavours – Pinot Grigio, unoaked Chardonnay (e.g. Chablis), Garganega (Soave) and Chenin Blanc.

The second go-to branch for sensational summer sipping is CITRUS FRUITS, which boasts vibrant varieties that are dripping with zesty fruit flavours and vivacious acidity, providing excellent matches for delicate seafood and seasonal salads: Grüner Veltliner, Falanghina, Sémillon and dry Riesling.

The wines across both of these branches are usually unoaked and fruit forward – they also taste of sunshine and good times!

The summer 'spotlight' grapes are unoaked Chardonnay (Orchard Fruits) and dry Riesling (Citrus Fruits), both being 'noble' or well-known, widely planted 'international' grape varieties. They are covered in more detail in the autumn and winter sections respectively.

Orchard Fruits

UNOAKED CHARDONNAY
(pronounced: Shar-don-ay)

Chardonnay is adept at expressing its terroir – or sense of place – and nowhere is this more true than in its birthplace of Burgundy in eastern France – one of the greatest wine regions in the world.

Within Burgundy is the Côte d'Or (meaning Golden Slope), which includes the Côte de Nuits and the Côte de Beaune (for more on this region turn to autumn, p. 180). To the north of that is Chablis and to the south is the Côte Chalonnaise and Mâconnais:

- (Champagne)
- Chablis
- Côtes de Nuits (part of the Côte d'Or)
- Côte de Beaune (part of the Côte d'Or)
- Côte Chalonnaise
- Mâconnais
- (Beaujolais)

Also found in
French wine regions outside of Burgundy – such as the Languedoc-Roussillon and Limoux – and throughout the wine-producing world. Pretty much every country produces Chardonnay, from China to Chile, Spain to South Africa and Turkey to Tasmania.

CHABLIS

As a region Chablis is cold and consequently the wines are dry, taut and steely with high acidity. This elegant, distinct style of Chardonnay is usually unoaked, which might explain why many people who think they hate Chardonnay love Chablis!

There are four different quality levels of Chablis and they are Grand Cru (of which there are seven), Premier Cru, generic village-level Chablis and then Petit Chablis, which is a good, cheaper alternative.

At the opposite end of Burgundy from Chablis are the Côte Chalonnaise (e.g. Montagny) and Mâconnais regions, which encompasses Mâcon, Mâcon-Villages and wines such as Pouilly-Fuissé and St-Véran. Whites from here are also largely unoaked (and made from Chardonnay) but are far riper and softer in style – because they are further south – than the slightly more austere Chablis.

Flavour profile

Ranges from the coolest, crispest styles like Chablis, which display notes of nuts, honey and apple, to the riper styles found elsewhere, from Mâconnais to the Margaret River in Australia. These tend to boast riper notes of melon, banana and apricot.

Food and occasions

Lighter wines pair brilliantly with sushi, seafood, oysters, scallops and white fish, poached salmon, salmon fishcakes and a warm chicken or Caesar salad. Riper styles can cope with a bit more weight and flavour, such as crab linguine, salmon rillettes and hard cheeses. This is the ideal bottle to pop into a smart picnic hamper for enjoying at an outdoors cultural event.

Affordability £–££££

There is a Chardonnay out there for everyone and without having to pay for any oak influence, the unoaked examples can be good value – as long as you aren't planning on splurging on a Chablis Grand Cru!

Cool climate = wines that are tighter, more restrained and have higher acidity

DID YOU KNOW? It is said that it was the wife of the Emperor Charlemagne who insisted that white grapes be planted in their vineyards in Burgundy as she had had enough of looking at the red wine stains on her husband's white beard!

PINOT GRIGIO
(pronounced: Pee-no gridge-ee-oh)

Pinot Grigio is the Italian name for the French grape Pinot Gris (which hails from Burgundy but flourishes in Alsace, on the border with Germany). Pinot Grigio is grown throughout Italy, but the majority of plantings tend to be in the north of the country, in the Veneto region, as well as Friuli-Venezia Giulia, Lombardy and Alto Adige.

Also found in

One of the most popular grape varieties on the planet, Pinot Grigio is grown throughout the winemaking world and can be found in many Eastern European countries such as Hungary, Romania and Moldova as well as in Australia, Chile and South Africa. In Germany it is known as Grauburgunder and, in its guise as Pinot Gris, is found in Alsace and the Rest of the World, with notable plantings in the United States (Oregon) and New Zealand too, with some of these styles being slightly off-dry.

Flavour profile

Neutral, unobtrusive, subtle wines that have delicate aromas of nuts, honeysuckle and pear, although the more expensive bottles will have greater concentration of both flavour and structure. As a rule of thumb, if 'Pinot Grigio' is on the label, expect a slightly lighter, more restrained style of wine; if it says 'Pinot Gris', expect a wine that's riper and more tropical.

DID YOU KNOW? The French name 'Pinot Gris' derives from the fact that the grapes have a slightly grey/brown/pink tinge to them – hence the suffix 'gris' or grey.

Food and occasions

If you're planning an Italian meal then seafood pasta, risotto or a simple white fish will all match well, although given the tendency of this grape towards neutrality, it also complements light, delicate dishes such as no-fuss summery salads, nibbles, antipasti and cheeses (feta or mozzarella). Pinot Grigio is the ultimate 'festival' wine for a host of reasons: it's usually closed with a screwcap so there's no need for a fiddly corkscrew; it doesn't matter if it gets a bit warm as it has a natural freshness and acidity to it anyway, and there aren't lots of complex aromas to worry about losing if you're drinking it out of a paper cup.

Affordability £–££

Given the fairly ubiquitous nature of Pinot Grigio it can be picked up for a song – result!

CHENIN BLANC

(pronounced: Shen-in blonk)

A French variety from the Loire Valley, it is famous for producing a range of different styles, from sparkling Crémant to very sweet pudding wines, but a common feature of them all is taut, crisp acidity and notes of honey, apples and straw. The acidity helps to balance the sweetness in the richer styles and also gives them remarkable longevity. The dry wines are mainly single varietal and come from many appellations within the Loire Valley, but those of particular note are Savennières, Vouvray, Anjou-Saumur and Touraine.

Also found in

South Africa – where it is also known as Steen – Argentina and the United States.

Flavour profile

Loire Chenin has fairly brisk acidity (to put it mildly) with notes of honey, apples and straw and tends to be unoaked. Examples from the Rest of the World are softer, the acidity is lower and the fruit is riper with additional tropical fruit flavours vying for attention. Oak might be used too, imparting spiced apple and custard aromas.

Food and occasions

Lighter, fresher styles: the tangy apple flavours work really well with pork, in the same way as apple sauce complements roast pork. Salads, seafood and pretty much any fish also pair well, and the grape's acidity can cut through different dressings and sauces. It also works with egg-based dishes such as a quiche or frittata. Riper styles (including oaked ones) are a great alternative to Chardonnay, offering a similar structure and fruit flavours, but with higher acidity. Pair with roast chicken, meaty fish, lobster or a tropical but savoury salad such as mango and prawn. Chenin is marvellously multi-functional in that the wines can be enjoyed on a meat-free Monday with a frittata in the garden or with a simple salad that has just been rustled up, or even on the beach, kept chilled in a cooler, with that acidity being wonderfully refreshing under the glare of the sun. It even matches well with turkey, so don't forget to consider Chenin if you're celebrating Christmas in warmer climes!

Affordability £–£££

The lightly oaked wines are more expensive but you can get some really great value, juicy, fruity Chenin, especially from South Africa. The French wines tend to be a bit pricier.

GARGANEGA
(pronounced: Gar-gan-ey-ga)

Garganega is an Italian grape from the Veneto region and the principal variety found in Soave, where it can be blended with other ones including Verdicchio.

Also found in
Native to Italy.

Flavour profile
Garganega produces almond-scented wines with hints of melon, pear and apple coupled with crisp acidity. Some prestigious producers use oak for their top wines but this is highly unusual.

Food and occasions
If you're going down the complement route, enjoy with ceviche, white fish, poached chicken or a simple green salad. If you want to try the contrast route, Garganega (Soave) works surprisingly well with richer dishes such as seafood pasta or risotto, as the acidity cuts through the richness. Open a bottle on a summer's evening when entertaining friends, when the warmth of the sun has just begun to fade, and serve alongside seafood linguine or ravioli.

Affordability £–££
Garganega (Soave) is widely available, cheap to buy and makes a great alternative to Pinot Grigio.

SUMMER

MELON DE BOURGOGNE

(pronounced: Mel-on duh Borg-oyne)

Melon de Bourgogne is a French variety responsible for making Muscadet and is grown in the Loire Valley, with the most notable appellation being Muscadet-Sèvre et Maine.

Also found in
There are also some plantings in North America but it is pretty much exclusive to Nantes, in the western part of the Loire Valley.

Flavour profile
A little like champagne, a number of these wines are made 'sur lie' – remember, that's when the wines are given extended 'lees contact' with the dead yeast cells to add extra interest. These wines can be quite tangy (almost salty) and dry with notes of apple, citrus and pear.

Food and occasions
These wines are famously superb with oysters so ideal for a romantic evening at home.

Affordability ££
A good value French white wine that is widely available.

Citrus Fruits

DRY RIESLING
(pronounced: Reece-ling)

This German grape variety was once believed to make the greatest white wines in the world (hence its status as a 'noble' grape variety) but it's rather fallen out of fashion, replaced by French grape varieties such as Chardonnay and Sauvignon Blanc. The dry (or *trocken*) Rieslings are produced throughout the country and there are thirteen main wine regions including the Mosel which arguably produces the archetypal German style of Riesling: delicate, floral and with high acidity.

Also found in
Riesling is a hardy vine that is suited to cool climates. It is also grown in Alsace (France) – with the best wines coming from the Grands Crus vineyards – and neighbouring Austria, notably in the Wachau region. There are also plantings in Eastern Europe, North America, Canada, Chile and New Zealand. In the Rest of the World, Australia, in particular, has carved out a reputation for making superlative Riesling especially from the Clare Valley, Eden Valley and Tasmania.

Flavour profile
Riesling produces wines with quite high acidity and low alcohol. Those from the Mosel region have pretty floral notes, which are from flavour compounds called monoterpenes. These include linalool (violets and lavender) and geraniol (rose). Austrian Riesling is generally a bit riper and peachier, whereas examples from Alsace tend to be citrus scented with notes of grapefruit, lime and lemon.

In Australia the wines share the same wonderful acidity but also have distinctive notes of violets (just like Parma Violet sweets) and lime. With time in bottle they also develop a unique note of kerosene or petrol due to the flavour compound with the catchy name: TDN or 1,1,6-Trimethyl-1,2-dihydronaphthalone. Riesling is always unoaked and is rarely blended.

Food and occasions

Dry Riesling (or just off-dry as opposed to sweet) is a fantastic match with seafood (especially prawns), subtly flavoured white fish or salmon. It works well with pork, Mexican food (think tuna tacos or pulled pork) but also with lighter Thai and Vietnamese noodle-based dishes that are less sauce-led – think Pad Thai. Try a bottle next time you have a ready meal or takeaway at home or go to your favourite Thai restaurant. The lower alcohol levels also make Riesling a refreshing lighter wine to drink at lunch or for sipping poolside.

Affordability £–£££

Though still on the more affordable side of things, Riesling is certainly not as cheap as it once was – but what is? The cheapest wines are still from Germany; prices increase as you go up through the quality levels and also if you head Down Under.

DID YOU KNOW? Dry Riesling is largely, qualitatively, a very different animal to the medium-sweet German blends such as Hock, Blue Nun and Liebfraumilch.

SÉMILLON
(pronounced: Sem-e-on)

Sémillon (no accent outside of France!) is a French variety from Bordeaux, where it is commonly blended with Sauvignon Blanc and is an important component of the sweet wines too, such as Sauternes.

Also found in

Australia, particularly in the Hunter Valley, produces some really excellent dry wines capable of great longevity, as does the Barossa Valley and Margaret River. Historically South Africa also embraced the grape, though other whites have since taken precedence and are significantly more popular to plant. You'll also find producers in both North and South America, as well as New Zealand and Eastern Europe.

Flavour profile

Sémillon can at times be quite reminiscent of Sauvignon Blanc with fresh, green notes, but usually it is riper, fleshier and more textured, with classic flavours of lemon, lower acidity and a wonderful waxy quality. With time in bottle it can develop distinctive and utterly delicious notes of toast, wax and honey.

Food and occasions

A superlative match for seafood, fish, sushi or salads, but the waxier texture also gives it the body to marry with richer foods like chicken dishes. It's sensational with summer's seasonal vegetables – think fennel, green beans or courgettes with lemon. The richer, riper styles are great with slightly more robust dishes – creamy sauces, salmon en croûte or a Parma ham and mozzarella salad.

Affordability ££–£££

Not the cheapest but reasonably priced and worth seeking out.

GRÜNER VELTLINER
(pronounced: Groo-ner velt-leaner)

Grüner Veltliner is Austria's premier white grape variety and the main wine regions include Kamptal, Kremstal and Wachau. Austria's wine classification is extremely similar to Germany's with the best wines being DAC (Districtus Austriae Controllatus).

Also found in:
Grüner Veltliner is also grown in Europe – especially Eastern Europe – and New Zealand.

Flavour profile
Grüner makes dry, fresh, unoaked wines that taste of citrus – both lemon and tangerine – but also white pepper, herbs and spice (which doesn't come from oak but from the grape). The best wines can also have an appealing roundness and texture to them, especially if yields are kept low.

Food and occasions
Grüner Veltliner pairs really well with the classic Austrian dish wiener schnitzel, but in the Southern Hemisphere it's often enjoyed with lighter Asian fare. It pairs well with artichokes and is excellent with 'buffet' food! From salads to cold meats and quiches, this is your superlative summer fête or street party wine.

Affordability ££
A slightly esoteric choice but one that will reward you with a zesty, citrus-laden wine ideal for summer, that is surprisingly good value. Largely available for under a tenner.

FALANGHINA
(pronounced: Fal-ann-geaner)

A fabulous Italian white grape variety that comes from the region of Campania in the south, where it loves the volcanic soils and sunshine.

Also found in
Native to Italy.

Flavour profile
The wines can be quite an attractive lemony gold in colour with aromas of bitter orange and citrus blossom. They are unoaked and fruity and riper examples can have a suggestion of yellow plums.

Food and occasions
A great match with summer staples: seafood and salads. The lemony nature of the wine will also work beautifully with anything that has been cooked or marinated in citrus, and cut through slightly richer, even salty sauces such as the anchovies in a Caesar salad. Since this is an Italian wine, we obviously can't omit pasta, so try it with a simple pasta pesto or (apparently Stanley Tucci's favourite) spaghetti alla nerano: spaghetti with courgettes.

Affordability ££–£££
Taking into account the rarity of this varietal, it's astonishing that it is as affordable as it actually is, with a fair few available on the high street.

OTHERS

There are a number of other grape varieties that are a good fit for the Citrus Fruits branch of the Wine Flavour Tree, being both zesty and fresh with lemon and lime acidity. Noteworthy examples include:

Assyrtiko, a Greek grape variety from the island of Santorini, renowned for its minerality and tight, citrus acidity which is well-balanced by white stone fruit flavours such as apricot.

Cortese (Gavi's grape) is Italian and the wines are unoaked, fresh and textured, making them fabulous with fish and seafood, the acidity acting like a squeeze of lemon.

In France, Picpoul de Pinet (made from the Piquepoul Blanc grape) is found in the Languedoc region and is increasing in popularity, favoured for its zesty freshness.

Portugal's Vinho Verde is an archetypal summer wine. Meaning 'green wine', this refers to the fact that it is released early when it is still very young and most have a subtle spritz to them.

DID YOU KNOW? Vinho Verde is a DOC in north-west Portugal that used to predominantly make red wines. Today it is primarily known for white wine production and there are a number of white grape varieties that may go into the blend: Alvarinho, Arinto, Avesso, Azal, Loureiro and Trajadura.

SUMMER WINE STYLES

Reds

When it comes to summer reds, SOFT & JUICY wines are a great option, as they are low in tannin but high in fruit, making them ideal for popping in the fridge and chilling to enjoy with meatier fish such as tuna or even a lighter chicken dish. Chilling a red highlights the structure of the wine but slightly compromises the fruit, so it's best to chill a red that doesn't have too much tannin or alcohol but lots of juicy, fruity aromas and flavours.

For bigger, bolder barbecue reds, turn to the BLACKBERRIES & SPICE branch of the Wine Flavour Tree in the winter section of the book (p. 225).

The flavours that you are likely to find in this style of wine are lighter red berry fruits such as strawberries and redcurrants, along with almonds and, unusually, banana! Banana is classically found in wines made the from the Gamay grape and the younger, juicier Beaujolais wines, in particular and those made using 'carbonic maceration'. Other varieties on this branch of the Tree include Cinsault, Dolcetto and Tarrango.

Soft & Juicy

GAMAY
(pronounced: Gam-ay)

Gamay is synonymous with one wine region in the world: Beaujolais in France, where it is best known for producing juicy, fruity wines ideal for chilling – such as the younger Beaujolais Nouveau and cheaper, entry-level wines. Some more 'serious' wines are produced too from ten 'Crus' (such as the beautifully named Saint-Amour), with Beaujolais-Villages straddling the two different styles.

The extremely fruity aromatics of the juicier styles isn't just down to the Gamay grape, it's also caused by a winemaking method called **carbonic maceration**. This is when the whole grape bunches are put into a fermentation vessel and the weight of the grapes crushes those at the bottom. These then split open and start to ferment in the usual way and the fermentation releases carbon dioxide as a by-product. This rises up and blankets the intact grapes above, which then go through an **intracellular fermentation**, i.e. the berries are kept whole and ferment with no skin contact, which means low tannin and colour.

Also found in
Gamay is grown elsewhere in France – the Loire Valley, Mâconnais and Gaillac – but also in Switzerland and, to a limited extent, the rest of the world – mainly the United States, Australia and Canada, with a couple of delicious examples coming out of New Zealand.

Flavour profile

The softer, juicier styles are extremely youthful in colour – almost purple – light in structure and with beguiling, fruity aromatics – think bubblegum, banana and strawberry. The more traditional 'Cru' wines taste of red and black cherries along with raspberries.

Food and occasions

Gamay is delicious served chilled with fish – a salad niçoise – or tomato pasta, but it's also wonderful with rustic French fare such as duck rillettes, charcuterie, pâté or soft cheese with a warm baguette. Grab a cool box or esky for your wine and food, a picnic blanket and a towel and go wild swimming.

Affordability ££–£££

These cheerful, easy-to-drink gluggers aren't terribly pricey but Beaujolais is becoming increasingly fashionable, with many producers in the region embracing the natural wine movement. Expect to pay more for the Cru wines.

REMEMBER The distinct aromas and flavours – such as banana and bubblegum – of younger, juicier wines made from the Gamay grape are as much down to the carbonic maceration winemaking technique as the grape variety.

DOLCETTO
(pronounced: Doll-chet-oh)

Dolcetto – meaning 'little sweet one' – is an Italian grape variety found to the north of the country, in the region of Piedmont. There are seven DOCs, including Alba and Asti, so a label might read Dolcetto d'Alba or Dolcetto d'Asti, indicating which village the grapes were grown in.

Also found in
Australia and the United States.

Flavour profile
Think cherries and berries with strawberries, cranberry and a suggestion of violets. Dolcetto can produce quite deeply coloured wines but with soft tannins and, compared to many Italian red grapes, relatively low acidity, which makes the wines approachable and soft, ready for easy and early drinking.

Food and occasions
A great match with charcuterie, Dolcetto also marries well with tomato-based pasta dishes, pizza, vegetables and garlic. It's a wine that works really well slightly chilled in the summer time when it's still young and vibrant and the acidity can cut through the fat of a juicy burger or a hot dog.

Affordability £££
Not widely found on the supermarket shelf, but all good independents will have a bottle and it's absolutely worth seeking out this gem.

CINSAULT
(pronounced: San-so)

A French grape variety typically used as part of a blend, both in Provence and also as one of the thirteen grape varieties permitted in Châteauneuf-du-Pape.

Also found in
In South Africa, the indigenous grape variety Pinotage is a cross between Cinsault and Pinot Noir but juicy, single varietal Cinsault is also found.

Flavour profile
The colour is light and youthful with flavours that are fresh and juicy: strawberries, wild strawberries, red cherry and raspberry along with soft tannins.

Food and occasions
This is another red wine that's terrific served chilled! Cinsault is extremely similar to Beaujolais and so it pairs well with the same sort of foods – rustic picnic fare and charcuterie – but you could also enjoy it with a steak and salad. It's a great wine to serve to a wine aficionado friend as they may not have come across it before, so hopefully it will surprise and delight them!

Affordability ££–£££
Not widely available, so it's no surprise that the pricing is mid-level plus, although Cinsault can increasingly be found in some supermarkets and independents.

Soft & Juicy styles are ideal for chilling during the summer months, as chilling highlights the tannins in red wines but can flatten fruit intensity so reds need to be soft and fruit forward to start off with.

TARRANGO
(pronounced: Ter-an-go)

Tarrango is a little known and rather unusual Australian grape variety that is a hybrid of Touriga Nacional and Sultana.

Also found in
Native to Australia.

Flavour profile
Light, bright, almost neon pink/light red in colour, with exuberant summer pudding aromas and flavours, fresh acidity and low tannin. Juicy, fun and fruity!

Food and occasions
Tarrango is essentially a red wine masquerading as a rosé! Enjoy with seafood, grilled halloumi, baked feta, vegetables or a simple Caprese salad. This is very much your mid-week 'me time' wine to take outside while you stick your feet in a paddling pool to cool down or just put them up full stop. Grab a magazine or newspaper, relax, take a deep breath and a minute for yourself. The wine will stay fresh in the fridge for a good few days so there's no need to share!

Affordability ££
A juicy, fun, summer-friendly wine that isn't especially complex or 'distinguished' but is all the better for that very reason!

SUMMER FOOD AND WINE MATCHING

When it comes to summer, wine is all about refreshment, relaxation and enjoyment and as meals become lighter and more delicate, so your summer wines need to reflect this. From seafood suppers, salads, picnics and, of course, the ubiquitous summer barbecue, there really is a wine out there for every dish. Lively, citrus-scented or subtle whites with more restrained flavours along with rosé and reds taken out of the fridge to enjoy with meatier fish are ideal. Dining becomes temporarily but wonderfully al fresco, and with that comes an ease of entertaining, as wines are popped into ice buckets and sipped through lazy afternoons and into leisurely evenings with friends and family.

There is such an abundance of wonderful seasonal ingredients, but there are a couple of things that I particularly look forward to in the summer months. Firstly ripe, sweet tomatoes in an array of colours, which are so versatile as they work just as well in salads – such as a Caprese salad – as in a simple but tasty tomato pasta sauce (mine is as easy to make as it is enjoyable!) And then there's corn on the cob, the ultimate summery side dish. Whether you pop it on the barbecue or boil it on the hob, adding a Mexican-inspired topping elevates it to new levels of deliciousness and helps it to take centre stage even when served with prawn tortillas and avocado salsa (aka guacamole).

Finally, summer wouldn't be summer without a salad, and two of my favourites are Lemon Chicken Salad and the classic Provençal Tuna Niçoise.

What's in season in the summer?

HERBS
basil, chives, dill, mustard greens, sage, tarragon, thyme

SALADS
chicory, lettuce, radishes, rocket, tomatoes, watercress

GREEN VEGGIES
artichoke, broad beans, broccoli, celery, courgettes, cucumber, fennel, green (or French) beans, kale, leeks, mangetout, marrow, peas, runner beans, samphire, sorrel, sweetheart cabbage, Swiss chard

MEAT
beef, duck, lamb, quail, rabbit, venison

OTHER VEGGIES
aubergine, beetroot, butternut squash, cabbage, carrots, cauliflower, garlic, mushrooms, new potatoes, onions, peppers, sweetcorn, white cabbage

FRUIT
apricots, blackcurrants, bilberries, blueberries, cherries, damsons, gooseberries, greengages, nectarines, peaches, plums, raspberries, redcurrants, rhubarb, strawberries

FISH AND SEAFOOD
brill, cockles, crab, dover sole, hake, herring, langoustine, lemon sole, lobster, mackerel, monkfish, mullet, oysters, plaice, red mullet

FOOD TYPE	BEST WINE TYPES: Citrus Fruits, Orchard Fruits and Soft & Juicy
Herbs:	Falanghina, Garganega, dry Riesling, unoaked Chardonnay
Salads:	Chenin Blanc, Dolcetto, Falanghina, Garganega, Pinot Grigio, dry Riesling, rosé, Sémillon, Tarrango, unoaked Chardonnay
Green veggies:	Sémillon
Other veggies:	Dolcetto, Tarrango
Fish and seafood:	Chenin Blanc, Falanghina, Garganega, Gamay, Pinot Grigio, dry Riesling, Sémillon, Tarrango, unoaked Chardonnay
Meat (inc. poultry):	Chenin Blanc, Cinsault, Garganega, dry Riesling, Sémillon, unoaked Chardonnay

SUMMER RECIPES

Pasta al Pomodoro – 166

—

Lemon Chicken Salad with Bacon
and Avocado – 167

—

Mexican Prawn Tortillas with Avocado Salsa
and Grilled Sweetcorn – 168

—

Grilled Tuna Steak Niçoise – 170

PASTA AL POMODORO

This dish always brings back the fondest of memories: holidaying in Italy and eating a bowl of pasta at lunch while sipping a glass of refreshing Falanghina. Swapping the pasta for courgetti will make this gluten-free.

+ WINE A juicy, subtle, lemony Falanghina is a match made in heaven, but an Italian Pinot Grigio or Soave would be an excellent choice too, with their pared-back flavours and fresh acidity. If you're looking for a red then a (chilled) Dolcetto has the necessary acidity to work well with the tomatoes – divine!

SERVES 4

3x tbsp olive oil
2x cloves of garlic, finely sliced
2x 400g fresh tomatoes, halved (Isle of Wight tomatoes are my favourite if you can get them – so tasty)
Salt and pepper
3–4 oz (85–115g) dried pasta per person (such as penne or tortiglioni – I like a tube for this dish)
Plenty of Parmesan (for a vegan dish, omit or serve with a vegan alternative)
4x courgettes if making courgetti

Heat the oil over a medium heat in a frying pan and fry the sliced garlic, taking care not to burn it. Add the tomatoes, a sprinkle of salt and a good grind of black pepper and gently simmer on a low heat until the tomatoes are really soft and sweet, around 20–30 minutes, breaking the skins down with the back of a wooden spoon. Add more olive oil if required – the tomatoes take a lot of oil!

Cook the pasta according to the instructions – usually around 12 minutes. Drain and serve, spooning the sauce on top with plenty of grated Parmesan.

If using courgettes instead of pasta, spiralise (or cut into ribbons with a peeler or mandoline) and then cook on the hob in a pan or wok over a medium heat with a knob of butter or olive oil for 1–2 minutes until ready.

LEMON CHICKEN SALAD WITH BACON AND AVOCADO

This was a firm summer favourite when I was growing up and it's easy to see why – it's simple yet delicious with plenty of flavour but a cinch to make.

+ WINE Something really tangy and lemony but with a bit of structure would be sensational with this salad as the citrussy notes of the wine would enhance those of the food. Therefore an Australian Semillon or Austrian Grüner Veltliner with their classic notes of lemon would marry well. If you'd prefer something with a bit more texture then a riper Chenin Blanc from South Africa would also be fabulous.

SERVES 4

2x tbsp olive oil
4x chicken breasts, cut into cubes
6x rashers of bacon, cut into 1cm pieces
Juice of a lemon
1x small handful of tarragon, chopped
100g broad beans, podded
1x large bag mixed salad leaves
2x ripe avocados

French vinaigrette:
1x tsp Dijon mustard
2x tbsp white wine vinegar
6x tbsp olive oil

First make the vinaigrette. Simply measure out the ingredients into a small jar, season and then shake to combine. Put aside.

Heat the oil in a frying pan and cook the chicken and bacon over a medium heat. Once they are starting to take on some colour, add the lemon juice and the chopped tarragon. Continue to cook until the meat is cooked through – if you're not sure, take a chicken piece out and cut in half to check.

While the meat is cooking, steam or boil the broad beans for a couple of minutes, drain, cover with cold water and, once cool enough to handle, peel the outer skin from each.

To serve, put the salad leaves into a salad bowl, slice the avocado and add along with the broad beans, chicken and bacon, finally pouring over the salad dressing. Combine and serve.

MEXICAN PRAWN TORTILLAS WITH AVOCADO SALSA AND GRILLED SWEETCORN

Mexican food is so joyful and colourful and the succulent sweetcorn adds a nice seasonal twist to the tortillas.

+ WINE This zingy, lime-drenched dish would be incredible with a lime- and orange-scented dry Riesling. Try a bottle from one of Australia's best regions – the Clare or Eden valleys. Alternatively, for a bit or residual sugar and riper fruit, enjoy a Pinot Gris made across the water in New Zealand.

SERVES 4

For the prawn tortillas:
450g raw shelled prawns
1x lime, juice and zest
1x garlic clove, crushed
2x tbsp olive oil

For the grilled sweetcorn:
4x corn on the cob
A small knob of butter for each corn
1x small pot crème fraiche (200 ml)
3x tbsp mayonnaise
1x handful fresh coriander, chopped (plus some to scatter on at the end too)
¼x tsp chipotle or sweet paprika
1x lime, juice and zest
100g feta cheese, crumbled

For the avocado salsa:
4x ripe avocados
½x red onion, finely chopped
1x red or green chilli, very finely sliced (can add individually at the end if wanting to avoid serving to children)
1x handful of fresh coriander, finely chopped
2x tomatoes, deseeded and finely chopped
2x limes – juice and zest
Salt and pepper

4x large plain flour tortillas

For the prawn tortillas:
Place the prawns in a small bowl and marinate in the juice and zest of the lime, crushed garlic and olive oil. Set aside.

For the corn-on-the-cob:
Cook the corn in a saucepan of boiling, salted water for around 8 minutes. Drain and put a knob of butter on each piece of corn.

While the corn is cooking, mix together the crème fraiche, mayonnaise, coriander, chipotle or sweet paprika, lime and feta.

For the avocado salsa:
Cut the avocado flesh into small pieces and put in a bowl with the red onion, chilli (if using), coriander, tomato, lime (juice and zest) and seasoning.

Now you're ready to assemble the dish. Fry the marinated prawns in a little olive oil over a medium heat for a couple of minutes and warm the tortillas in a microwave for about 15 seconds. Place them on a plate and add the prawns, followed by the avocado salsa along with a scattering of coriander leaves. Finally, spoon the creamy feta dressing over the sweetcorn and serve.

GRILLED TUNA STEAK NIÇOISE

Another summer staple at my house! There are a few elements to cook and assemble, but it's worth the effort – this is a stunning salad, especially when served on a large white platter.

+ **WINE** There is quite a lot of flavour going on in this dish, so Provençal rosé makes an exquisite wine pairing. The wines tend to be quite subtle in flavour but the acidity works brilliantly with the olives, dressing and beans. For a classic white wine, select an unoaked Chardonnay, such as a Chablis, as the acidity cuts through the richness of the fish and also marries well with the vinaigrette. Another great option is a chilled red – a Gamay, Tarrango or South African Cinsault – as lighter red wines love meaty fish like tuna.

SERVES 4

500g new potatoes, halved
4x eggs
220g French beans, trimmed
4x tuna steaks (tinned tuna works well too and is a cheaper alternative)
1x tbsp olive oil
A handful of small tomatoes, halved
A handful of black olives, pitted and halved
½ x red onion, finely sliced
A large bag of mixed salad leaves
12x fresh anchovies

French vinaigrette:
1x garlic clove, crushed
½x tbsp Dijon mustard
1x tbsp red wine vinegar
4x tbsp olive oil

Heat a large pan of salted water and cook the potatoes for 5 minutes before adding the eggs, and hard boiling them for 10 minutes, before removing from the water with a spoon. Place in a small bowl filled with cold water. Check the potatoes are cooked (use the tip of a knife), drain and set aside. Peel the eggs when they are cool enough to handle, then quarter.

Meanwhile, steam the green beans for 5–7 minutes until cooked.

Make the vinaigrette by mixing all of the ingredients together in a small jar and shaking. Season if desired.

Season the tuna steaks with salt and pepper. Heat a frying or griddle pan over a medium heat and add the olive oil and then the tuna, cooking on each side for 2–3 minutes maximum, according to the thickness of the steak. You want the tuna to be cooked on the outside but a little pink inside. Even a really thick steak can still have a nice pink middle after only 3 minutes but don't forget that it carries on cooking once removed from the heat so don't be tempted to leave it for any longer.

The salad is now ready to assemble. Dress the salad leaves and serve on individual plates or onto a white platter. Scatter all of the ingredients on top, including the tinned tuna if using. If you have used tuna steaks, leave them until last. Place one steak on each plate but if using the platter, slice the tuna into pieces and place on top. Serve immediately.

OTHER SUMMER WINE STYLES

Rosé Wines

While rosé can of course be enjoyed all year round, there is no doubt that the majority of wine drinkers consider it to be a summer drink. It is usually light, fresh and uncomplicated and so suits the relaxed mood of summer. Even though colour wise the wines are pink, they are delicate in terms of aroma and flavour wise could easily be mistaken for a wine from the Orchard, Citrus Fruits or Soft & Juicy branch of the Tree, with their subtle flavours overlaid with a suggestion of red fruits. These delicate red fruit flavours come from the short period of skin contact that the juice has before being drawn off the skins and being made like a white wine (see p. 46 for more information on rosé winemaking). Indeed, rosé has more in common with white wines than red.

The depth of colour of a pink wine tends to indicate how flavourful it will be, although not how sweet. In the same way that golden-hued wines are likely to have more personality than water-white ones, which are typically lighter and fresher, paler rosé wines are usually more restrained in aroma and flavour. This stands to reason because the paler the colour, either the less time the juice spent on the skins of the red grapes or the more delicate the grape variety.

Pale rosé – although not ultra-pale 'vin gris' rosé – is indisputably extremely fashionable, especially those from the French region of Provence. Here the weather is dry, sunny and windy (due to the Mistral wind) and so a lot of the grapes can be grown organically. The region's largest appellation is Côtes de Provence, although there are also four designations that can append their name to this: Fréjus, La Londe, Pierrefeu and Sainte-Victoire. Common varieties include Mourvèdre, Grenache, Cinsault and Syrah.

Indeed, rosé is made from many different grape varieties grown in many different regions throughout France, not just Provence, from Bordeaux to Beaujolais, the Loire and the Rhône, where Tavel rosés made predominantly from Grenache produce wines that are deeply coloured and full of flavour. Loire rosé tends to be crunchier due to the Cabernet Franc grape and Bordeaux pinks can be a bit leafy with cherry fruits. They are all subtly different and nearly always dry.

In Italy, 'rosato' Pinot Grigio can produce affordable, easy-drinking wines with a range of different sugar levels, but distinctive pinks include the beautifully coloured Cerasuolo d'Abruzzo (quite bright and vibrant) made from Montepulciano. Further south, wines are also deeper in colour and more characterful – such as those made from Negroamaro and Nero d'Avola – while the further north you go, the lighter both in colour and body they tend to get as the climate isn't as warm and sunny.

For characterful and beautifully coloured rosé, Spanish 'rosado' is hard to beat, especially from the Navarra region and from wines made from Garnacha. Rioja, though famous for its reds, also produces pink wines made predominantly from Garnacha and Tempranillo.

Rosé wine is produced throughout the winemaking world and excellent examples are being made in England (predominantly from Pinot Noir), as well as further afield in the Rest of the World. In the United States off-dry styles such as White Zinfandel and White Grenache are popular as well as dryer wines. Historically the word 'blush' used to be used for very pale rosé wines and then for these sweeter styles, but it is rarely used nowadays and if it is, it is simply interchangeable for generic rosé rather than a specific style.

Autumn

INTRODUCTION

The nights are drawing in, growing colder and darker; children have gone back to school and routine has returned . . . autumn has arrived. The exuberance and freedom of summer recedes and with it the social whirl and heady feeling that pervades the long, lingering evenings and outside events. Even if Indian summers mean that early autumn can still be warm, we tend to retreat indoors more, away from the encroaching chill. Crops are gathered in, leaves start to fall and as our Earth tilts away from the sun, the desire for comfort and for warmer, heavier, richer foods inevitably starts. Autumn's fare – such as root vegetables and game – suits the season and dishes such as soups and risottos are ideal for these increasingly colder months. As meals become more substantial, their accompanying wines need to become more structured, to match the style and weight of these heartier dishes. While wines aren't as big and rich as they are in winter, they are nevertheless medium- to full-bodied – often with soothing notes of spice and vanilla oak – and reds are more often pulled from the rack than whites, certainly Chez Caporn.

The new season is not only buoyed by the arrival of different, delicious seasonal foods but is also peppered by religious events like Diwali – where the triumph of light over dark is celebrated – and cultural festivals such as Thanksgiving, celebrated predominantly in Canada and the United States. In very early autumn the colourful, exuberant and joyful Sydney Gay and Lesbian Mardi Gras Parade takes place and Australia and New Zealand also celebrate Anzac Day, a day of remembrance that commemorates the landing of troops in 1915 in Gallipoli, Turkey.

Culturally though, the key occasion celebrated around the world in autumn is Halloween (unless you're in the Southern Hemisphere). The origins of this festival are Celtic, 'Samhain', when it was believed that souls returned to their homes and so people wore costumes and built fires to ward off spirits. This isn't dissimilar to Mexico's Day of the Dead – Dia de los Muertos – an uplifting festival when ancestors and friends who have died are remembered and toasted with a glass of their favourite beverage. In England, Scotland and Wales, Guy Fawkes Night has been marked in November for over 400 years, with fires lit and fireworks exploding across the sky to commemorate the foiling of an assassination plot against King James I in 1605. Participants head outside in gloves, scarves and woolly hats to join together for a last social hurrah before Advent, with many evenings ending with a massive bowl of warming chilli con carne and a generous glass of red wine.

WHAT'S HAPPENING IN THE VINEYARD?

While summer saw the berries change colour and start to ripen, with the grapes getting bigger, sugars accumulating and acidity decreasing, autumn sees the harvesting of the grapes get underway. This is typically in the months of September and October in the Northern Hemisphere and February and March in the Southern, with the grapes being picked either by hand or by machine, before making their way to the winery to begin the winemaking process.

AUTUMN WINE STYLES

Whites

In autumn, the zingy citrus and elegant Orchard Fruit whites (not to mention pinks) of summer are replaced by wines with more weight, body, texture and alcohol. The structure of the wines increases the further you go up the Wine Flavour Tree, and now we are on the penultimate white branch: STONE FRUITS.

This branch offers up Chardonnay, Viognier, Albariño and Fiano, united in their offering of peach and apricot aromas and flavours along with notes of nectarines and yellow plums. The riper fruit flavours make these varieties a superb match with autumn's sweeter, starchier root vegetables such as butternut squash as well as with chicken tagines or fish pie.

This season's 'spotlight' grapes are Chardonnay and Merlot, both French 'noble' varieties that remain among the most widely planted and enjoyed in the world. As ever, the varieties are ordered according to how widespread both plantings and availability largely are.

CHARDONNAY
(pronounced: Shar-don-ay)

The most popular and most planted international white grape, Bourgogne (or Burgundy in English) is the French birthplace of the Chardonnay grape. Its parents are Pinot Noir and Gouais Blanc – Chardonnay was the result of a spontaneous cross (when a grape is bred from two different varieties when the flower of one is fertilised by the pollen of another) in the vineyard – and the finest wines come from the Côte de Beaune sub-region of the Côte d'Or.

The Côte de Nuits, on the other hand (to the north of the Côte de Beaune), is famous for its red wines made from Pinot Noir and both regions are also well known for their pre-historic Jurassic limestone soils. Within the Côte de Beaune are found such illustrious villages as Meursault and Puligny and Chassagne-Montrachet, to name but a few. It is these village names that will be found on the label rather than Chardonnay, due to regional labelling.

There are four different quality levels when it comes to the wines of the Côte de Beaune and these are:

- **Grand Cru:** the top of the quality tree, there are eight Grand Crus of which seven produce white wines only – made from Chardonnay – such as Montrachet and Corton-Charlemagne
- **Premier Cru:** the level below Grand Cru, there are forty-two of these, including Meursault Premier Cru (there is no Grand Cru for Meursault) and Puligny-Montrachet Premier Cru
- **Village:** e.g. Meursault, Puligny-Montrachet
- **Regional:** e.g. Bourgogne Blanc (can put Chardonnay on the label)

South of the Côte de Beaune is the Côte Chalonnaise, which includes villages such as Montagny and Rully, and then finally the Mâconnais whose star villages include Pouilly-Fuisse (not to be confused with Pouilly-Fumé in the Loire Valley, which produces Sauvignon Blanc) and Saint-Véran.

Outside of Burgundy, Chardonnay is grown elsewhere in France, notably in Champagne (for sparkling wine production) and in the Languedoc-Roussillon.

Chardonnay from around the world emulates the top wines of Burgundy, which are regarded as the absolute pinnacle of what can be made from this variety.

(See unoaked Chardonnay on p. 142 for information on Chablis.)

DID YOU KNOW? Some consumers still believe that Chardonnay is synonymous with the now unfashionable, almost sweet seeming, full-on tropical fruit-bomb style of wine that was prevalent in the 1990s. It was this version of the grape that gave rise to the expression 'ABC': Anything But Chardonnay. However, given the enormous range of styles that can be produced from this one variety, there should be a Chardonnay out there to suit everyone.

Also found in

Chardonnay is made in a vast number of wine regions globally, from England to Australia, and has a great ability to let both the winemaking and paradoxically the terroir shine through at the same time. Here are some of the very best regions where this most ubiquitous of white grapes can be found:

- **Europe:** Chardonnay is widely grown throughout Europe, such as in the Jura region of France, in Eastern Europe, Italy (usually the cooler regions of the north-east but also Sicily) and Spain, such as in Somontano.

In England while most Chardonnay plantings are for sparkling wine production, some excellent still wines are also being made.

- **Australia:** produces a range of styles at different prices. The very best are from cool-climate regions such as Tasmania, the Adelaide Hills in South Australia and Margaret River in Western Australia, with great value wines made in South East Australia where Chardonnay may be blended with other varieties such as Semillon.
- **New Zealand:** although it's better known for its pungent Sauvignon Blanc, it's absolutely worth checking out New Zealand's fabulous Chardonnay, from the North and South Islands alike: Hawkes Bay, Waiheke Island and Gisborne.
- **South Africa:** making simply sensational Chardonnay, look for regions such as Stellenbosch, Hemel-en-Aarde Valley and Walker Bay.
- **The United States:** California produces fantastic Chardonnay, especially in Napa, Sonoma, Carneros, Santa Barbera, Monterey and Oregon. The mid-priced wines can be rich, ripe and buttery but the pricier ones are likely to be more elegant.
- **South America:** look for the Uco Valley and Limari on the label.

Flavour profile

Chardonnay is capable of extraordinary versatility and as such is found twice on the Tree (see pp. 15 and 30): on the Orchard Fruits branch, where it is unoaked and lean with notes of apple and honey, and on the Stone Fruits branch, where the flavours are richer, riper and redolent of peach and apricot, especially in wines from warmer regions.

In between these two styles can be found many other expressions of the grape, all dependent on factors such as climate and winemaking. However, given its natural predisposition to neutrality, certainly in cooler climate regions, the most delicious and prestigious wines – and those that garner the higher price tags – tend to use oak fermentation and/or ageing for a suggestion of spice, typically using French oak as the resultant flavour is more subtle. Some of the riper Stone Fruit styles might be oaked or unoaked, with the latter simply having gone through a stainless steel fermentation.

There is often a roundness and softness to the majority of Chardonnay as they usually go through malolactic fermentation which also lends a buttery flavour to the wines.

Food and occasions

Given the medium-bodied weight and structure of Chardonnay and its relatively unobtrusive flavours coupled with fresh acidity, it's a great wine match for a wide range of dishes: meatier fish or lobster, creamier fish recipes (gratins and fish pie), risotto, carbonara pasta, roast chicken, chicken pie and even cheeses. If in doubt when it comes to fish and poultry – as long as it's not spicy – Chardonnay can pretty much be your default wine option. It's also a classic match with root vegetables. As such it can be enjoyed at a number of different occasions from a girls' night in to a cosy book club meet, a Sunday lunch to a smart dinner party. If you are celebrating Thanksgiving, it's also a great match with turkey!

Affordability £–£££££

Because Chardonnay is made in such a wide range of styles from all around the world, there is a wine for every price point and palate, from large-scale production wines made in the Central Valley of Chile or across Australia, to the auction-worthy Grand Cru wines of Burgundy and the premium-priced examples of the Rest of the World.

VIOGNIER

(pronounced: Vee-on-yay)

Viognier originates from France's northern Rhône and is the grape variety that makes up the wines of both Condrieu and the tiny appellation of Château-Grillet. It can also be co-fermented – when more than one grape variety is fermented together at the same time – with Syrah in the wines of Côte Rôtie, giving a delicate, perfumed lift. From the northern Rhône it travelled to the Southern Rhône and the Languedoc-Roussillon, where it is commonly blended with other white Rhône varieties such as Marsanne, Roussanne, Grenache Blanc and also Chardonnay.

Also found in

Aside from its homeland in the northern Rhône and further afield in France (which has the most plantings worldwide), Viognier is also grown in California. Here the Rhône Rangers – producers heavily influenced by the wines and varieties from the region – enthusiastically adopted it. Australia, and Barossa (South Australia) in particular, have also really made this variety their own with some fine organic wines too. Elsewhere there are also excellent examples coming out of South Africa, Chile and New Zealand.

Flavour profile

With its golden colour, waxy, full-bodied, almost oily, viscous texture, relatively high alcohol, low acidity and heady notes of ripe peach, apricot and nectarine, it is undeniably both distinctive and delicious. If you imagine the smell of a peach yoghurt, you are pretty much there!

Food and occasions

With its distinct notes of peach and apricot and its breadth and depth in the mouth, Viognier is superb with Middle Eastern dishes such as tagines and couscous – especially those that contain apricot, no surprise! Milder curries are also excellent, such as a korma or a Pad Thai, as are autumn's root vegetables. Viognier is the quintessential cosy white and is a superb choice for curry nights in or movie nights on the sofa: it's also a great match with popcorn!

Affordability ££–££££
Viognier can be snapped up at a fairly reasonable price, though it does tend to hover around the mid-range, with many of the cheaper examples coming from other regions in France and also Australia. Wines from the illustrious region of Condrieu, however, are considerably more expensive.

ALBARIÑO
(pronounced: Al-ba-reen-yo)

Albariño is from Galicia, in north-west Spain, and Rías Baixas in particular – a coastal region as it likes to be cool – and also neighbouring Portugal, where it is known as Alvarinho. 'Albar' means white, and 'ño' or 'nho' usually refers to smallness.

Also found in
Uncommon outside the Iberian Peninsula, but it can occasionally be found in Australia, South Africa, New Zealand, the United States and Uruguay.

WINE FACT Albariño is labelled varietally, unlike wines from other Spanish regions such as Rioja or Toro.

Flavour profile

These wines burst with alluring notes of apricot, peach and nectarine, but they also have crisp lemony acidity and a certain saline quality, too, which is thought to come from the close proximity to the sea.

Food and occasions

Sensational with fish and seafood, especially more robust dishes such as black squid ink risotto, fish stews, crab linguine or scallops with parsnip or cauliflower purée. It can also be matched with lighter meat such as chicken. This fashionable wine is your ideal Indian summer/early autumn choice as it beautifully combines the peachy medium-bodied profile of autumn with the zesty citrus notes of summer. For me it's the ideal bottle to drink outside at a weekend lunch with friends, grabbing a warm jumper and candles as the sun starts to set but being warmed by a steaming bowl of rice or pasta. It's also great to enjoy over a wide assortment of different tapas, either at a bar or at home.

Affordability ££–£££

You can't find 'cheap' Albariño – I suspect because it is not widely grown – with the (quite rare) oaked examples being even pricier, as time spent in oak always adds to the cost.

WINE FACT It was discovered in 2009 that most of the Albariño being grown in Australia was actually the French Savagnin (different to Sauvignon Blanc) grape, as the wrong cuttings had been sent overseas by mistake.

FIANO

(pronounced: Fee-ah-no)

This sultry, southern Italian variety from the Campania region produces some excellent medium-bodied, slightly textured, almost waxy wines, especially from the Fiano di Avellino DOCG and from Sicily.

Also found in
Plantings are increasing slightly in Australia and in Argentina.

Flavour profile
Expect classic Stone Fruit flavours of apricot and apricot kernel but also honeysuckle and orange. Alongside the appealing aromatics is a palate-pleasing texture.

DID YOU KNOW? While Fiano is usually drunk while it is very young, its texture, weight and balance will allow for it to improve in bottle for a few years.

Food and occasions
Fiano is another grape variety that has an affinity with seafood and fish, but choose something with some weight and texture to marry that of the wine, such as a chowder or a rich salmon (smoked or flaked) tagliatelle. Alternatively, try a classic autumnal butternut squash risotto, veggie lasagne or a savoury tart with a scattering of sage. For meat lovers, Fiano is ideal with a chicken or ham pie or other types of pork such as chops. Draw the curtains or close the blinds, pour a glass of wine, pop some music on and enjoy the wine right through from meal preparation to sitting down at the table. This is your mid-week superstar.

Affordability ££–£££

A bit like Albariño, Fiano is usually mid-range BUT there are some great supermarket own-labels being made at the moment, which means it is available at discounters and on the high street too. Increasingly affordable.

OTHERS

There are two other white Rhône grape varieties that, along with Viognier, display some of these stone fruit characteristics and they are Marsanne and Roussanne. Both are the only two varieties allowed in the whites from such illustrious northern Rhône (usually red wine) appellations such as St-Joseph, Hermitage and Crozes-Hermitage, whereas only Roussanne is allowed in white Châteauneuf-du-Pape. Roussanne has a slight russet tone to its skin and aromas of herbs along with apricot kernel and peach. Marsanne, like Viognier, is ripe, textured and full-bodied with floral notes and flavours of pear, apricot and quince.

The lesser-known Spanish variety of Godello – grown in north-west Spain and Portugal – also displays the Stone Fruit peachy notes from this branch of the Wine Flavour Tree.

AUTUMN WINE STYLES

Reds

Similarly to autumn whites, the reds move up a gear from the lighter, fresher styles of summer, to wines that pack a bit more of a punch in terms of both flavour and structure, with medium-bodied-plus varieties providing more in the way of texture and alcohol too. Autumn wines are arguably the ultimate people pleasers. The reds are comforting, velvety wines, smooth and succulent, with plump fruits and little in the way of hard tannic edges. You'll find them on the BERRIES & CHOCOLATE branch of the Wine Flavour Tree.

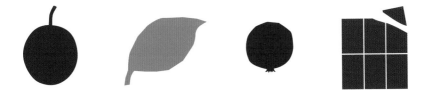

This branch boasts varieties such as Merlot, Tempranillo, Barbera and Nero d'Avola, and Tempranillo, in particular, is often swaddled with seductive spicy oak notes that carry the comfort factor even further. While these wines match well with weightier dishes, their fruit-forward nature also means that they can be enjoyed on their own, while cooking or snuggled up on the sofa in front of the TV.

MERLOT
(pronounced: Mehr-low)

Merlot is an indigenous French grape variety that is now so popular internationally that for many wine lovers, its origins might not even be known. Like Cabernet Sauvignon it is a Bordeaux native and does, in fact, rather play second fiddle to its slightly more sophisticated half-sibling Cabernet, in terms of both global plantings and popularity.

In Bordeaux, these two red varieties are separated by the Gironde Estuary and the rivers Dordogne and Garonne, and while Cabernet calls the Left Bank home and is the dominant variety in the famous – and ludicrously expensive – First Growths, Merlot's home is the Right Bank, where it is typically the main staple of the wines of St-Émilion and Pomerol.

On the Right Bank, the gravel soils of the Médoc make way for a variety of different soil types including clay, which Merlot prefers, and here – unlike the historical 1855 classification from over the river – the classification of the wines of St-Émilion is regularly revised, the last revision having taken place in 2022.

- **St-Émilion Premier Grand Cru Classé A:** Château Figeac and Château Pavie. Châteaux Angelus, Ausone, Cheval Blanc all decided to withdraw from the classification
- **St-Émilion Premier Grand Cru Classé B:** awarded to twelve châteaux
- **St-Émilion Grand Cru Classé:** awarded to seventy-one châteaux

In neighbouring Pomerol, wines are also made predominantly from Merlot.

DID YOU KNOW? Merlot is the second most planted red grape in the world after Cabernet Sauvignon.

Although Merlot can make single varietal wines of distinction, it is frequently found as part of a blend along with Cabernet Sauvignon and Cabernet Franc – a 'Bordeaux blend'. Merlot brings stuffing and upfront fruit to the party, Cabernet Sauvignon structure and an ability to age and Cabernet Franc a certain lift, perfume and pencil lead fragrance.

Also found in

Although widely found throughout its homeland of Bordeaux – including the regions of Blaye, Bourg and Fronsac, which all offer good value – Merlot is pretty much grown everywhere in the winemaking word, including China and Turkey. Outside of the rest of France and Europe (notably Italy) it is widely grown in the Southern Hemisphere:

- **California:** still very popular even if it has rather fallen out of favour and been supplanted by Cabernet.
- **South America:** for many years there was some confusion in Chile as to whether some vines were Merlot or Carménère.
- **South Africa:** especially Stellenbosch
- **New Zealand:** where some first-class Bordeaux blends are made, notably around Hawke's Bay and Australia.

Flavour profile

Merlot produces quite large berries with relatively thin skins, which results in wines that are softer and more approachable than Cabernet Sauvignon. Flavour wise expect plums, blueberry, black cherries and chocolate – and often spicy notes, too, from time spent in oak.

Food and Occasions

Given the easy-going, fruity and fleshy nature of Merlot, this is pretty much a party wine! Great for crowd-pleasing occasions, it can be enjoyed with finger foods such as olives and charcuterie or served with a steaming bowl of chilli (beef or bean) after the fireworks.

Affordability £–£££££

There is literally a Merlot on the market for every budget, with cheap, cheerful and easy-drinking mass-market examples available on supermarket shelves, premium artisan offerings and, of course, those stellar wines from Bordeaux for those with extremely deep pockets.

TEMPRANILLO

(pronounced: Temp-ran-e-oh)

Tempranillo is the third most planted red grape variety in the world, after Cabernet Sauvignon and Merlot, but it hasn't quite enjoyed their international success and is still very much associated with one country: its homeland, Spain. The grape is synonymous with one region in particular, and that is Rioja – pronounced Ree-o-kah – which is found in the north of the country near Logroño and is named after the local river: Rio Oja. As ever in 'Classic Europe', the wine is named after the region, rather than the grape variety. The dominant grape in this popular red blend is Tempranillo, which is usually blended with Garnacha (Grenache) and two lesser-known varieties – Mazuelo and Graciano.

Elsewhere in Spain exceptional wines are made from Tempranillo in Ribera Del Duero and Toro (both found in the Castilla y León region), where Tempranillo is known as Tinto Fino and Tinta de Toro respectively.

Also found in

Known as both Tinta Roriz and Aragonez in Portugal – where it is a key component of port – there are also plantings in the warmer regions of Argentina, Australia, Chile and the United States.

DID YOU KNOW? In Spanish 'temprano' means 'early'; Tempranillo is an early ripening variety.

Flavour profile

The predominant fruit flavour of Tempranillo is that of plums, but there are also notes of cherries and brambles. However, due to the fact that many wines are aged in oak – some for a number of years – the fruit flavours tend to co-exist with those of spicy oak and notes of leather and cedar from time spent in bottle. This is known as bottle age.

One of the most distinctive things about Rioja is the use of oak, and I think that the soft, spicy notes that it imparts are key to the wine's immense popularity. Both American and French oak are used, with American oak being more traditional, though increasingly both are used together. Remember, wines that have used American oak tend to display notes of coconut, vanilla and dill whereas French oak adds spicier aromas and flavours such as nutmeg and cinnamon. Cheaper examples and some fruit-led wines will be unoaked, in which case the fruit flavours shine through more.

When buying Rioja, it is important to know what certain terms mean on the label, so that you can understand why some bottles are more expensive than others. The words 'Crianza', 'Reserva' or 'Gran Reserva' indicates the minimum amount of time that the wine has to have had in both barrel and bottle:

- **Crianza wines** = 1 year barrel and 1 year in bottle minimum
  = 2 years ageing total
- **Reserva wines** = 1 year barrel and 2 years in bottle minimum
  = 3 years ageing total
- **Gran Reserva wines** = 2 years barrel and 3 years in bottle minimum
  = 5 years ageing total

Food and occasions

Tempranillo is your archetypal 'hug in a mug' sort of wine: no hard edges and all plush fruit and spice. It is a great match – like Merlot – with warming lasagne or pizza but also mushrooms, lamb cutlets, shepherd's pie, pork and, of course, paella! In fact, Rioja works brilliantly with saffron, so try a tagine too. Soft and delicious, the versatile Tempranillo can be enjoyed with a meal – either as a mid-week treat or as a Saturday 'splash out' depending on the quality of the wine – or simply as a fabulous fireside red.

Affordability £–£££

Tempranillo can be found across a range of price points, from juicy, fruity gluggers to the world-class examples found in Spain's most illustrious regions.

WINE FACT Primary aromas are those that come from the grape variety itself, secondary aromas are the result of the winemaking process (such as the use of oak) and tertiary aromas are from time spent in bottle as the wine ages.

BARBERA

(pronounced: Barb-air-a)

Like Nebbiolo, Barbera is a northern Italian grape; in fact, it's the most widely planted red variety in the region of Piedmont.

Also found in

Barbera has made its way from Italy to the other side of the world, notably to Australia, Argentina and the United States, though plantings are small compared to those of Italy.

Flavour profile

A slightly under-the-radar Italian red that isn't as well known as Sangiovese (Chianti) or Nebbiolo (Barolo or Barbaresco) but encapsulates all that is most delicious about Italian wine, with oodles of black cherry and plum fruit along with refreshing acidity. It also tends to be quite deep in colour with soft tannins.

Food and occasions

With its brisk acidity and vibrant fruit, Barbera makes a great match with tomato-based sauces – think pizza and pasta – mushrooms, rich meat dishes, sausages and even hard cheeses. Italians pretty much only drink wine with food, and Barbera is a great wine for enjoying with a rustic, robust, slow-cooked meal, wolfed down after a chilly weekend walk.

Affordability ££–£££

Despite its drinkability, Barbera is not actually thought of as an illustrious variety in Italy, although it's certainly easier on the wallet than wines such as Barolo and Barbaresco. Having said that, some impressive examples are made, with the best coming from the DOC regions of Alba and Asti, in particular Barbera d'Asti DOCG, which will cost more.

NERO D'AVOLA
(pronounced: Ner-oh de ave-o-la)

This southern Italian variety is largely found in Sicily, which is just as well as it really likes the sunshine!

Also found in
It is rarely seen outside of Italy but there are minuscule numbers of plantings in California, Malta and the warm Riverland area of Australia.

Flavour profile
Nero d'Avola produces wines that are medium- to full-bodied, rich and plummy, with relatively high levels of alcohol, colour and a lot of purple fruit flavours such as from plums. Also expect black cherries and blueberries – along with tobacco leaf notes.

Food and occasions
This is not a shy and retiring grape variety and it doesn't go with shy and retiring foods! It is at its best with charcuterie, caponata, pasta al norma (aubergines with tomatoes and fresh basil), creamy tomato pasta dishes and braised red meats. These robust but succulent wines are terrific mid-week wonders, wonderful with a warming bowl of pasta or a juicy burger.

Affordability ££
Good value; these wines tend to be quite easy on the wallet.

AUTUMN FOOD AND WINE MATCHING

When it comes to pairing different wines from the Stone Fruits branch of the Tree with appetising autumnal dishes, start by taking a look at the fresh, seasonal produce that is widely available, such as root vegetables, cabbage and mushrooms; vegetables also have the added benefit of not being too expensive either. For red wines, it's a good idea to think about the weight of the food you fancy at this time of year as even if it's available all year round (think beef), chillier days call for warming plates of food.

Personally, I'm usually quite time strapped so I like to make meals that are straightforward and create as little washing-up as possible. My autumnal recipes therefore feature a classic soup (easy, cheap and flavourful), which is a triumph with a lightly oaked Chardonnay or apricot-scented Viognier; a 'one-pan wonder' risotto (I'm called the Risotto Queen in my family) that will work just as well with a fresher white or red, so long as they both have acidity; a cosy fish pie (back into Chardonnay territory) and another one-dish wonder, the classic post-fireworks favourite – chilli – for which you just need to add a smooth, fruity red.

What's in season in the autumn?

HERBS
chervil, coriander parsley, sage, sorrel, thyme

SALADS
chicory, rocket, tomatoes, watercress

GREEN VEGGIES
broccoli, Brussels sprouts, celeriac, chard, fennel, kale, leeks, mangetout, peas, runner beans, spinach

OTHER VEGGIES
artichoke, aubergine, beetroot, butternut squash, carrots, cauliflower, celery, courgettes, garlic, marrow, mushrooms, pak choi, parsnips, peppers, potatoes, pumpkins, radishes, red cabbage, shallots, swede, sweetcorn, turnips, white cabbage, wild mushrooms

FRUIT AND NUTS
apples, blackberries, chestnuts, damsons, pears, plums, quince, raspberries, redcurrants

FISH AND SEAFOOD
anchovies, bream, clams, cockles, cod, crab, haddock, hake, lobster, mackerel, monkfish, mussels, oysters, plaice, pollack, prawns, red mullet, sardines, scallop, sea bass, skate, squid

MEAT
beef, chicken, duck, goose, grouse, guinea fowl, hare, lamb, partridge, pheasant, pork, quail, rabbit, venison

FOOD TYPE	BEST WINE TYPES: Stone Fruits and Berries & Chocolate
Herbs:	Albariño
Salads:	Barbera, Chardonnay, Fiano, Nero d'Avola, Viognier
Green veggies:	Tempranillo
Other veggies:	Barbera, Chardonnay, Fiano, Merlot, Nero d'Avola, Tempranillo, Viognier
Fish and seafood:	Albariño, Chardonnay, Fiano
Meat (inc. poultry):	Barbera, Chardonnay, Fiano, Merlot, Nero d'Avola, Tempranillo, Viognier

AUTUMN RECIPES

Butternut Squash Soup with Crisp
Sage Leaves – 202

—

Posh Fish Pie – 203

—

Porcini Mushroom and Truffle Oil Risotto – 204

—

Chilli Con Carne with Shredded Beef – 206

BUTTERNUT SQUASH SOUP WITH CRISP SAGE LEAVES

You can't beat a quick, easy soup on a cold day and this one looks, smells and tastes like autumn. The cream is a must for that extra deliciousness so try not to swap it out for a low-fat option.

+ WINE A lightly oaked Chardonnay with subtle spicy notes from the oak and a rounded texture will work beautifully with the creamy structure of the soup. Alternatively, an apricot-scented Viognier with its viscous structure and succulent fruit is a great match.

SERVES 4

- 2x tbsp olive oil
- 1x red onion, finely chopped
- 2x packets of ready sliced/prepared butternut squash (around 385g–400g a pack or 2x whole squash cut into 2cm cubes)
- 750ml vegetable stock (use less if you like a really thick soup)
- A good grind of pepper and a sprinkle of salt
- Sage leaves – around 5 per person
- 125ml double cream

Heat the olive oil in a large pan and gently fry the onion and the chopped squash until they have started to soften, about 10 minutes.

Add the stock along with the seasoning, bring to the boil and simmer for a further 10–15 minutes until the veggies are totally soft.

Meanwhile, heat about a teaspoon of oil in a frying pan on a medium heat and cook the sage leaves until crispy – making sure they don't burn. Cool to crisp up further.

When the squash is soft, turn off the heat, stir in the cream and then blend, either with a hand blender or in a food processor or mixer. Serve the soup in warmed bowls, pop a few leaves of crispy sage on top and more pepper if required. This is delicious with warm sourdough.

POSH FISH PIE

This is a really delicious, decadent fish pie; it's a fabulous comfort dish for when the nights start drawing in and can be enjoyed throughout autumn and well into winter.

+ **WINE** A lightly oaked Chardonnay is absolutely terrific with fish pie as it has the weight and structure to match the creamy sauce and the potato topping. If you want to go down the contrast rather than the complement route, however, try a fish-friendly Albariño – although it is lighter in style and structure, it has enough body and texture to cope with the dish.

SERVES 4

For the mash:
5x large white potatoes
50ml milk
50ml double cream
40g butter

For the fish pie mix:
2x tbsp olive oil
1x medium onion, finely chopped
1x large carrot, finely chopped
150ml double cream
1x juice of a lemon
1x tsp English mustard
A good handful of medium Cheddar cheese
1x salmon fillet (no skin)
1x cod fillet (no skin)
100g frozen prawns, defrosted
100g frozen scallops, defrosted
Salt and pepper

Boil a saucepan of lightly salted water, peel the potatoes and cut them into equal-size pieces so that they cook at the same time – allow about 17 minutes. Once ready, drain and place a piece of kitchen roll over the colander to absorb excess moisture.

Preheat the oven to 200/180°C fan. Heat the oil in a large frying pan and fry the chopped onions and carrots for about 10 minutes, until soft, before adding the double cream. Give the mixture a good stir and then add the lemon juice, mustard and cheddar cheese. Season.

To make the topping: mash the potato with the milk, cream and butter; season with a sprinkle of salt and a grind of pepper.

Cut the fish fillets into cubes/large pieces and place the fish and seafood in an ovenproof, earthenware dish, pour over the creamy sauce and mix, then spoon the mash on top. Pop in the oven for around 30 minutes or until the potato topping looks golden and slightly crisp. Serve with steamed, buttered, seasonal Savoy cabbage.

PORCINI MUSHROOM AND TRUFFLE OIL RISOTTO

Risotto is one of the (very few) things that I can actually make better than my husband and I love the simplicity of the dish and how you don't need too many ingredients – just a bit of patience and a willingness to stand at the hob for a while! When it comes to matching wine with risotto you can either go down the 'complement' or the 'contrast' route.

+ WINE If you want to complement the creamy character of the risotto then pick a ripe, slightly buttery Chardonnay; but if you want your wine to act like a squeeze of lemon (I always serve my risotto with plenty of lemon) then you would want something a little fresher with higher acidity, like a Southern Italian Fiano. The zesty acidity will cut through the dish, refreshing the palate and making it ready for another mouthful. A final option would be an Italian Barbera – remember 'what grows together goes together' – as both truffles and Barbera come from Piedmont – and the vibrant acidity of the wine, even though it is red, will, like the Fiano, cut through the rich rice while also marrying well with the umami nature of the mushrooms.

SERVES 4

- 1x 30g jar of dried porcini mushrooms
- 2x tbsp olive oil
- 1x medium onion, finely chopped
- 2x cloves garlic, finely sliced
- 250gm chestnut mushrooms, roughly sliced
- 300g risotto rice
- 150ml dry white wine or vermouth
- 1l vegetable stock (you will also have some reserved mushroom stock, see method)
- A good grind of pepper and a sprinkle of salt to taste
- 1x tbsp of truffle oil
- 50g butter
- 80g grated Parmesan
- A handful of flat-leaf parsley, roughly chopped (optional)
- 2x lemons to serve (quartered)

Rinse the porcini mushrooms in a sieve (they can be gritty), put in a bowl and pour over 500ml of boiling water; soak for 20 minutes. When they are ready, sieve again, reserving the 'mushroom stock'.

While the dried mushrooms are soaking, chop the onions and slice the garlic and chestnut mushrooms, weigh out your rice, cut your butter into cubes, grate your Parmesan, make up the vegetable stock and chop your parsley if using.

Heat the olive oil in a frying pan over a medium heat, add the onions and soften for about 8 minutes, then add the sliced garlic and fry for a further couple of minutes before finally adding the prepared porcini and sliced chestnut mushrooms. Cook until the mushrooms have started to soften – about 5 minutes depending on the thickness of the mushroom slices. Now add the rice and dry fry for a couple of minutes before adding the white wine or vermouth – I simply add what I have open at the time; leftover rosé works well, too – and stir for a couple of minutes until the alcohol has reduced.

You are now ready to add the stock, a ladle at a time, adding the next ladleful once the rice has absorbed what is in the pan. Start with the reserved mushroom stock, along with a sprinkle of salt, and then move on to the vegetable stock. Turn the heat down a fraction – the rice will take longer to cook but it will cook more evenly. I always taste the rice as I go along (only after about 20 minutes or so) to make sure it is soft and cooked to my liking, I'm not a fan of chalky rice. I'd allow at least 40 minutes of stirring for the rice to be ready.

Once it is cooked, remove from the heat, drizzle over the truffle oil, check the seasoning and add the butter and parmesan, stirring well. Scatter the parsley on top and serve in warm bowls with the lemon quarters on the side. *Buon appetito!*

CHILLI CON CARNE WITH SHREDDED BEEF

The quintessential post 'trick or treating' or fireworks dish that just screams autumn! It's also easy to scale up if you're entertaining. Serve with basmati rice, sour cream or crème fraiche and a scattering of fresh coriander.

+ **WINE** Serve this rich chilli with a medium-bodied, smooth, succulent red from the Berries & Chocolate branch of the Tree but make sure it has lots of fruit to balance the spice of the dish. A juicy warm-climate Merlot, a rich, robust southern Italian Nero d'Avola with plenty of chocolate notes or a lightly spiced Crianza Rioja would be ideal. You want a wine that has plenty of flavour but no hard tannins as they will jar with the spice.

SERVES 6

2x tbsp olive oil
1x onion, finely chopped
2x tsp dried chilli flakes
2x tsp mild chilli powder
1x tsp unsmoked paprika
1x tsp ground cumin
1x tsp ground coriander
250g beef mince
250g braising steak, diced
1x 400g tin chopped tomatoes
250ml beef stock
1x 400g tin kidney beans, drained and rinsed
Salt and pepper
1x small bunch of fresh coriander, chopped

Heat the oil in a heavy saucepan over a medium heat and fry the onion until it starts to soften – this will take around 10 minutes.

Add the chilli flakes, chilli powder, paprika, cumin and coriander, stir well and then add the mince.

In a separate pan, brown the braising steak. When both meats are brown, add the braising steak to the other cooked ingredients, then add the tomatoes, beef stock and kidney beans. Season.

Cook on a low heat for two hours. When you're ready to serve, use a couple of forks to break up/shred the braising steak until the mince and steak are combined. Serve with the fresh coriander sprinkled on top.

OTHER AUTUMN WINE STYLES

Orange Wines

Orange wines are the quintessential autumn wine; not only does their amber colour reflect the changing landscape around us, as the leaves start to turn and fall, but they also have their own 'wine day' – National Orange Wine Day – in October no less! You can, of course, drink orange wines all year round, but with their broad texture and tannins, they suit autumn's richer dishes brilliantly.

What exactly are orange wines?

Orange wines are made from white grapes that are fermented like a red wine. The grapes are crushed and the juice is left to ferment in contact not only with the skins but also with the seeds and, less often, the stems. Sometimes a 'pre-fermentation maceration' also takes place (when the grapes and juice are left to soak together before the fermentation) which lasts around one to three days, but the magic really happens both during and after the actual fermentation. As a result of this extended skin contact, orange wines straddle both white and red wines in terms of style: their colour is somewhere in-between, they have structure and even tannins from the time spent on the skins that are reminiscent of red wines, but have aromas and flavours that are more on the white grape spectrum, although with greater depth and richness of flavour.

A brief history of orange wine

The term 'orange wine' was only coined in 2004 by a UK wine importer called David Harvey, but orange wines themselves have been produced for millennia and consequently they are very traditionally made. Originating in Georgia, this style has relatively recently been embraced by passionate advocates and winemakers in Europe – notably Italy (primarily in the north-east in Friuli-Venezia Giulia) and Slovenia – and more recently in the Rest of the World too, in Australia, New Zealand and South Africa. This is doubtless as a result of the resurgence in the popularity of orange wines over the last twenty to thirty years. Latterly, orange wines have become slightly more mainstream, with an increased presence on the shelves of independent wine shops, in many of the national supermarkets and also on the lists of wine bars and restaurants.

How orange wine is made

It is arguably the traditional, low-interventionist way of making orange wine coupled with their unique flavour profile that has (re-)ignited the interest of both winemakers and wine consumers. As previously mentioned, the harvested grapes are crushed and left in a large vessel until the wild yeasts – these are generally preferred over cultured yeasts – start the fermentation.

The most popular fermentation vessel for orange wines is the Georgian 'qvevri' – pronounced 'kevree' – the very first wine fermentation vessel ever used in the production of wine. Qvevri are essentially large pots or amphorae, reminiscent of large eggs, that are buried underground. Alternative fermentation vessels include open-topped oak vats so that the winemaker can punch down the floating cap of skins with a long stick – as happens in red winemaking – to keep it in contact with the fermenting liquid. This helps with both colour and tannin extraction and also with keeping the bubbling ferment at a consistent temperature.

Since producers of orange wines typically espouse the traditional winemaking methods, their approach is usually very 'hands off'. Once the fermentation has finished the majority of wines will go through malolactic fermentation and some will stay in contact with the skins for a further period of time – anything from a few weeks to a year or even more.

If so, the qvevri are likely to be sealed, sometimes with the addition of small amounts of sulphur to prevent oxidation, with the alcohol in the wine helping to gently extract more colour and tannin from the grape skins. Gradually, the skins, seeds and stems fall to the bottom of the vessel, passing through the wine, naturally filtering it, before the wine is moved to a different, clean vessel for ageing; this might be concrete, oak or even stainless steel. The longer the maceration or skin contact the longer the wine is likely to need to age post fermentation in order for it to soften.

Orange wines are made in a broad range of styles from relatively light and fresh to dark, chewy and tannic and the more robust styles need longer in barrel and/or bottle to show their true potential.

While orange winemakers are indisputably non-interventionist and the wines are made extremely traditionally or 'naturally', not *all* orange wines are natural wines. Some producers may choose to add cultured yeasts and the grapes might not be organic or biodynamic – both of which would prevent a wine from being a 'natural' orange wine but would still make it an orange wine. Many of the wines *are* natural due to shared sympathies but they are not necessarily so. Orange wines, like natural wines, also struggle with regulation and classification. Some countries (such as Italy) don't recognise orange wine as a category, although South Africa, for example, has created new legislation and labelling requirements for this relatively fledgling category, despite it being steeped in the traditions of the past.

Orange wine varieties

In Georgia, common grape varieties for orange wine include Mtsvane and Rkatsiteli, while in Italy Ribolla Gialla and Pinot Grigio reign supreme. Wines made from Pinot Grigio may also rather charmingly be referred to as 'ramato' – 'ramo' meaning copper – referencing the distinctive colours of the wine. Pinot Grigio as a grape has naturally slightly pink skins and so with extended skin contact this really becomes evident. Sauvignon Blanc and Semillon are popular in Australia and Rebula in Slovenia.

Winter

INTRODUCTION

Winter seems to elicit a wide range of emotions in people. In the Northern Hemisphere, the festive season begins with Advent in December, which brings the promise and then the cheer of Christmas, with carol singing, nativity plays, ice skating, mulled wine and Santa. As well as Christmas, other winter religious festivals include the Jewish festival of Hanukkah (which takes place over eight days) and Bodhi Day, a Buddhist festival that is also celebrated in some countries in the Southern Hemisphere.

For many, though, winter can be a struggle, with grey days and equally grey moods, although the sun is already starting to head back to us after the Winter Solstice; a cause for celebration for many around the world. It makes perfect sense to want to fill the dark with light; from candles to twinkling fairy lights and roaring fires. In Sydney, the Festival of Lights, aka Vivid Sydney, transforms the city for three weeks, running from late autumn to early winter, where colour and beauty require the dark to shine. In Québec, the Winter Carnival encourages participants to engage in fun and games with parades and activities, while in China, the Harbin International Ice and Snow Sculpture Festival – the largest in the world – takes advantage of winter's raw materials. For those who love winter sports, now is the time to don those skis or snowboards and enjoy the pristine slopes. New Year's Eve and Day also fall in the winter for many countries, along with Chinese New Year (January or February) and in the States there is Groundhog Day and the New Orleans annual Mardi Gras (meaning Fat Tuesday) and of course, Valentine's Day in February.

Aside from all of the religious and cultural events, cold, crunchy, frosty days can also be glorious though it's actually quite nice to have an excuse to head indoors and hole up too. Yes, winter does mean shorter and darker days, but being able to close the curtains by 5 p.m. can be really cosy! It keeps the outside world at bay and allows for a human version of hibernation as we slow down, replenish our energy levels and refuel with the heavier comfort foods of the season. With these fuller, richer, denser foods comes the need for more full-bodied wines – pretty much always red in my house – to match. The exception to this on the winter menu is game – pheasant, grouse, partridge, duck and venison – which demands something a bit more elegant with fresh acidity.

WHAT'S HAPPENING IN THE VINEYARD?

Harvest is over, the grapes are in and being made into wine, the leaves have fallen and it is now time for the vine to rest as it becomes dormant. For the vineyard workers, however, it is time for winter pruning, when the canes of the vine are cut back and new ones selected for when the growing cycle starts again come spring, with budbreak.

WINTER WINE STYLES

Whites

Winter whites can arguably draw on autumn's treasure trove of richer wines, as they match many winter dishes too – notably full-bodied, succulent, oaked Chardonnays or rich, viscous Viogniers.

But for spicier winter dishes such as curries and stir fries, these heavier dry whites don't work as well – you need aromatic, fragrant, exotic grapes instead. This is because they often have a bit of residual sweetness or sugar in them which serves as a great foil to the chilli and spice so often found in these foods. The branch of the Tree that boasts these sorts of grapes is the EXOTIC FRUITS & SPICE branch, bearing off-dry Riesling, Gewürztraminer, Torrontés and Muscat.

Along with Chardonnay (unoaked and otherwise), Riesling is the only other grape to appear on the Tree twice, so varied is the style of wines that this widely planted variety is capable of making. We've already seen dry Riesling in the summer section of the book as a 'spotlight' variety, where it is found on the Citrus Fruit branch of the Tree, so turn to p. 149 for further information on this fabulous variety.

OFF-DRY RIESLING
(pronounced: Reece-ling)

Riesling is an indigenous German variety and the purest expressions of the style are arguably found in the Mosel region, where the steep, slate soils help to ripen the grapes. When buying *dry* Riesling look for the word trocken on the label, but for *off-dry* wines search for feinherb (historically halbtrocken) or, for the best wines, Kabinett or Spätlese (just make sure it is without the word trocken next to it).

Also found in

Look to Alsace, France, for world-class Riesling too. Helpfully, since 2021 the label has to clearly show how sweet the wine is and so either you will find a sweetness scale on the back label or one of the following terms will be used:

- Sec – 4g/l RS or less – dry
- Demi-sec – 4–12g/l RS – off-dry
- Moelleux 12–45g/l RS – medium-sweet
- Doux – over 45g/l RS – sweet

In Austria, Kabinett or Klassik wines are dry, whereas Spätlese wines can have residual sugar in them.

Off-dry Riesling is also widely made in the Rest of The World:
- **Canada:** in all four regions: Québec, British Columbia, Ontario and Nova Scotia
- **United States:** in the Finger Lakes region a 'taste profile' can be found on the back of the bottle to indicate how sweet the wine is
- **Australia:** the Clare Valley and Eden Valley produce extraordinary Riesling, both dry and off-dry
- **New Zealand:** mainly in the cooler South Island

Flavour profile

The off-dry wines can be wonderfully aromatic, with flavours redolent of tropical fruits such as pineapple and mango as well as floral notes and a suggestion of spice – they are very much at home on the Exotic Fruits & Spice branch of the Tree.

Food and occasions

Off-dry Riesling is a match made in heaven with spicy food, from an Indian or Thai curry to spiced fish cakes, vegetables or even a spiced noodle salad, because the sweetness counters the heat of the spice. Instead of reaching for a chilled beer next time you enjoy spicy food at home, in the pub or at a restaurant, try a glass of off-dry white instead.

TIP As an alternative to off-dry Riesling, off-dry rosé is also delicious with spicy food and if you choose a really plump, soft 'smashable' red with no obvious tannins but plenty of ripe fruit, they can be good too.

Affordability £–££

Riesling is extraordinary value for the quality so this is very much a grape variety to get to know and love. German Riesling remains the best value overall as even great bottles can be very affordable.

GEWÜRZTRAMINER
(pronounced: Gur-vurz-tram-in-er)

The very Germanic-sounding Gewürztraminer actually heralds from the Alsace region in France, which is found to the north-east of the country and borders Germany and Switzerland.

WINE FACT Gewürztraminer is a variant or mutation of the grape Savagnin Blanc (NOT Sauvignon), which is the same variety – just a different name or synonym – as the Italian Traminer. You could argue, therefore, that the heritage of Gewürz is actually Italian even though it's widely regarded as being French.

Also found in
Germany and Italy, as well as many Eastern Europe countries such as Bulgaria, Hungary, Moldova, Romania, Slovakia and Slovenia. In the Rest of the World, Australia, Canada, Chile, New Zealand and the United States all make excellent examples of this distinctive variety.

Flavour profile
Gewürztraminer, or Gewürz (meaning perfumed or spicy), is arguably the easiest wine grape to identify blind in the world. It is a pretty gold in colour, intensely aromatic and smells of roses, hand cream, lychees and Turkish delight – it has even been described as smelling like 'a tart's boudoir'! Intensely perfumed and with a slightly viscous or oily quality, it also has quite low acidity levels. As ever with aromatic varieties, Gewürz can make both dry and sweet wines, with the latter ranging from just off-dry to the very sweet.

Food and occasions

Gewürztraminer is a good match with spicy food, such as Chinese, Indian or Thai, but also with really smelly cheeses! A classic 'what grows together goes together' pairing is with the Alsace cheese Munster. It also pairs with other strong cheeses such as Stinking Bishop or Époisses – it is one of the very few wines that can cope. So, next time you have a cheese and wine evening, or even a cheeky cheese fondue, try this unusual variety. It's also excellent if you are hosting a wine tasting because the aromas are so distinctive that most people should be able to smell the floral notes, courtesy of the flavour compound linalool.

Affordability ££–£££

The more affordable wines tend to come from the Rest of the World (Chile, for example), with the excellent Alsace wines – especially the Grand Cru – being pricier.

TORRONTÉS
(pronounced: Tore-on-tez)

Confusingly, there are three varieties of the Argentinian Torrontés grape, the primary one being Torrontés Riojano; the other two are Torrontés Mendocino and Torrontés Sanjuanino. Torrontés Riojano is widely grown in the Argentine wine regions of La Rioja and Salta.

Also found in

Torrontés' popularity has not really spread beyond Argentina, although it can be found in neighbouring Chile. There is also (rather unhelpfully) a Torrontés grape found in Spain but they are not related.

Flavour profile

The wines tend to be aromatic, fresh and lightly floral with white stone fruit and tropical fruit aromas. These wines are typically dry, although some have a suggestion of residual sugar.

Food and occasions

Torrontés and Thai food are a great combination; aromatic varieties go so well with spicy dishes, so it's also a good match for empanadas. Even though it is an aromatic grape variety it is quite fresh and flavourful, so Thai salmon would be an ideal partner. This is a great wine for serving if you are entertaining friends at home and want to give them something new to try, or take it to a BYO restaurant. It's also less distinctive than some of the other aromatic grape varieties so a good 'starter style'.

Affordability ££

Torrontés isn't the easiest to find on a supermarket shelf or wine list because it isn't widely grown but the wines tend to be mid-range in terms of price.

MUSCAT
(pronounced: Muz-cat)

Muscat is a French grape variety and while there are a number of different names ascribed to it, there are actually only two main Muscat varieties – Muscat Blanc à Petits Grains and Muscat of Alexandria (also known as Zibibbo). In France Muscat mainly produces dry wines from Alsace but also famous sweeties such as Muscat de Beaumes de Venise, a sweet but also fortified wine.

Also found in
Italy, Greece and Australia, in particular in the region of Rutherglen.

Flavour profile
Muscat is capable of producing a range of styles of wine from the dry to the very sweet and even sparkling such as Moscato d'Asti – Moscato is Italian for Muscat. All, however, are famously perfumed and aromatic as well as actually tasting of grapes! Muscat flavours can range from grapey and floral in both dry and sparkling wines to intensely honeyed with nuances of ginger and spice in sweet wines. The fortified styles have enthralling notes of raisins, treacle and black toffee, which makes them spectacular with Christmas pudding and mince pies!

Food and occasions
Another grape variety that is best drunk with either a lightly spiced curry or smoked fish such as salmon. This is an eclectic choice of wine, best enjoyed as part of a cosy dinner à deux either at home or at a specialist wine bar.

Affordability £££
The best dryer styles are from Alsace and consequently you'll pay a slight premium for these wines.

OFF-DRY PINOT GRIS

(pronounced: Pee-no gree)

Pinot Gris and Pinot Grigio are actually one and the same grape; Pinot Grigio is simply the Italian name of this French variety which is largely found in Alsace.

Also found in

Aside from Alsace and Italy there are also plantings in Hungary, Germany (called Grauburgunder), Oregon in the United States and New Zealand, where it can make both dry and off-dry styles of white wine.

Flavour profile

Pinot Gris tends to be riper and more opulent than Pinot Grigio – which is on the Orchard Fruits branch – with a distinctive fruit profile of orange and spice.

Food and occasions

Once again, spicy food is the order of the day, such as an Indian or Thai curry. So order a takeaway (or buy a ready meal), settle down on the sofa and put your feet up.

Affordability £££

While Pinot Grigio arguably produces the best value wine on the market today, expect to pay more for Pinot Gris as it is not quite as ubiquitous and the quality is generally higher.

WINTER WINE STYLES

Reds

When it comes to winter, red wine rules and this is absolutely the season where I want to enjoy rich, full-bodied, black-fruited bottles. The deeper and richer the wine, the higher the alcohol is also likely to be, which is quite warming and provides a broader texture. The branch of the Tree that has the biggest, boldest reds is BLACKBERRIES & SPICE, right at the top, with aromas and flavours of black pepper, blackberry, bacon and liquorice.

The grapes found on the Blackberries & Spice branch are Shiraz/Syrah, Malbec, Zinfandel and Pinotage, and despite them producing quite structured wines, they can also be succulent as they largely like warm climates and so produce wonderful winter warmers: wines packed full of fruit with a pleasing weight. Interestingly, these same qualities make them great for summer barbecues; the peppery nature of the varieties works well with grilled, smoky meats and sticky ribs are well balanced by the ripe, almost sweet-seeming flavours.

At the opposite end (pretty much) of the flavour and structure spectrum of the Wine Flavour Tree is the RED FRUITS & ROSES branch, which at first glance may seem entirely unsuited to winter, with its flavours of cranberry, raspberry, rose and red cherry.

However, the grapes found there – Pinot Noir, Grenache, Nebbiolo and Sangiovese – go brilliantly with classic seasonal dishes and winter meats such as partridge, pheasant and venison. The game season may start in autumn but it runs right through into winter and the wine's fresh acidity and crunchy red fruits help to lift and balance the gamey meat. These wines are also an excellent match with turkey and goose.

Winter's 'spotlight' grape is Pinot Noir, also known as the 'heartbreak' grape, as it can be quite tricky to grow.

Blackberries & Spice

SHIRAZ/SYRAH

(pronounced: Shear-az and Si-rah)

Syrah is yet another French grape variety and is widely known as Shiraz in the Southern Hemisphere, especially in Australia. Wines can be called either Syrah or Shiraz, with the former suggesting (as a rule of thumb) that the wine has been made in a more restrained, elegant style, and Shiraz indicating a richer, riper style. As Syrah, its home is in the vineyards of the northern Rhône, in villages such as Cornas and Côte-Rôtie – where it is co-fermented with Viognier – as well as Hermitage, St-Joseph and Crozes-Hermitage. In the southern Rhône the grape is often used as a component part of many blends, including Châteauneuf-du-Pape.

Also found in

There are Syrah plantings in the Languedoc-Roussillon (for wines such as Minervois) and Provence and it is also widely grown throughout Europe.

Shiraz, however, is very much at home in Australia, where James Busby, 'the father of Australian wine', is thought to have taken it in the early nineteenth century. The main regions include the Barossa Valley, McLaren Vale, the Hunter Valley and the Clare Valley.

In California, winemakers have a particular fondness for this red varietal, and South Africa also produces excellent examples.

Flavour profile

Syrah produces fragrant yet quite tannic reds that are capable of ageing for many years and that display aromas of black pepper, violets, liquorice and . . . bacon!

Notes of bacon aren't usually evident in Shiraz, however – instead, expect to find distinctive notes of mint, eucalyptus, blackcurrant, blackberry and even black cherry.

Food and occasions
Think rich red meats such as braised beef, roasts and stews or fleshy aubergines. Syrah or Shiraz are both excellent choices to go with your Christmas meal too as, taking flavour balancing into account, there are a lot of strong flavours on the Christmas plate and this varietal can cope with all the side dishes. This variety also works even if you're celebrating Down Under with barbecue fare on the beach. The softer Shiraz can also be enjoyed with a bowl of olives or a simple cheeseboard while playing chess or a board game.

Affordability £–£££
Produced across such a wide range of price points, it's possible to pick up bargain-basement bottles, but the more expensive ones will have better varietal purity. Expect to pay significantly more for wines from the prestigious Rhône appellations.

MALBEC
(pronounced: Mal-beck)

A French grape variety that has its origins in the region of Cahors in the south-west of the country, where it is also known as Côt or Cot, as well as the 'black wine of Cahors', where Malbec must make up at least 70 per cent of the blend. It is also grown in Bordeaux (where it is added like a touch of seasoning to the red wine blends) and the Loire Valley.

Also found in

Argentina – and the region of Mendoza, in particular – is the new home of Malbec, making rich, velvety, deeply coloured red wines, with a certain floral lift and fragrance. Malbec is also grown in Chile, though it is often used as a constituent part of the red blends rather than as a single varietal.

Flavour profile

While cheap Malbec can disappointingly err on the side of red fruits, well-made examples are bursting with dark, rich black berry fruits along with brambles, plums, black pepper and spice.

Food and occasions

Malbec and steak go hand in hand, which is fortunate, given the Argentinian love of beef! Red meat serves to soften the tannins in red wine and make them more approachable. Steak aside, pies, casseroles, empanadas, fajitas, sticky ribs and burgers are all great choices and for vegetarians, beetroot and aubergines – especially moussaka – work well. The softer versions of this variety can be enjoyed without food, though the denser, more complex bottles would be ideal to serve to guests coming round for a dinner party with a 'meaty main'. Given the popularity of steak on Valentine's Day, a rich, seductive Malbec could be just the ticket and the smarter bottles also make good gifts.

Affordability £–££

One of the great things about Malbec, apart from being delicious and drinkable, is that it is such good value. You should be able to pick up a bottle pretty cheaply though, as ever, the better examples will cost you more.

ZINFANDEL
(pronounced: Zin-fan-dell)

Zinfandel has proved to be something of a mystery over the years with its origins and parentage being much disputed and discussed. However, in the 1990s DNA testing finally proved that Zinfandel is one and the same as the Italian grape variety Primitivo and also the Croatian variety Tribidrag or Crljenak. As Zinfandel, however, it is known as being the all-American red that is capable of producing wines with high levels of alcohol and fruit, with older vines in particular making wines of great complexity and longevity. It thrives in warm climates and especially in the Californian region of Lodi.

Also found in
Zinfandel likes to be warm and so is found in the hotter regions of Southern Hemisphere countries such as Australia and South America. As Primitivo, it is found in the south of Italy, especially Puglia, 'the heel of Italy'.

Flavour profile
Zinfandel tends to burst with plump black fruit flavours along with notes of summer pudding, raspberry and apple. It also has noticeably high levels of alcohol.

DID YOU KNOW? Zinfandel is also used to make a distinctive medium-dry rosé called White Zinfandel.

Food and occasions

Red meat and robust reds are natural bedfellows and Zinfandel is no exception. Pair with brisket, slow-cooked shoulder of lamb, pork (especially sticky ribs) or a veggie burger. As Primitivo, try it with game, spicy tomato-based pasta dishes or pizza. Ribs and 'Zin' can be enjoyed whilst watching some sport on the TV or during a pizza night – either in or out.

Affordability ££–£££

Available in a range of price points, from soft and juicy gluggers to deep, rich 'old vine' examples made by world-class producers.

PINOTAGE

(pronounced: Pee-no targe)

Pinotage is a South African grape variety that is a crossing – created in the 1920s by Abraham Izak Perold – of two French grape varieties: Pinot Noir and Cinsault. It is widely grown throughout the country but is nevertheless only the third most planted red variety there after Cabernet Sauvignon and Syrah and makes up 6–7 per cent of plantings/area under vine.

Also found in

South Africa produces the lion's share of the world's Pinotage (about 98 per cent) but there are other plantings, predominantly in the Southern Hemisphere, in countries such as Brazil.

Flavour profile

Pinotage can make dense, rich, full-bodied reds when yields are kept low, boasting notes of black fruits, plums, blackcurrants and black cherry, with a certain smoky note to some of them. Oak will add notes of spice. Cheaper more commercial blends can boast red berry fruits as well as black.

Food and occasions

We have been known to barbecue in the winter months (my husband infamously cooked our Christmas turkey outdoors one year – we ate VERY late), and when I think of Pinotage I think of a Braai. The sometimes smoky nature of the wine pairs brilliantly with smoky meats of any description, along with venison, a tomato-based Indian curry or meaty mushrooms. Cheaper versions are ideal with mid-week meals such as sausage pasta, pepperoni pizza or stuffed Portobello mushrooms.

Affordability ££–£££

Cheap Pinotage is easily available at just over the £5 mark, but it can smell a bit like 'burned rubber' and so it's worth investing a little bit more if you can afford to, to really see what this grape variety is all about.

Red Fruits & Roses

PINOT NOIR
(pronounced: Pee-no nwar)

Pinot Noir is French and, like Chardonnay, is from the prestigious Burgundy region, which has a 'temperate, semi-continental' climate: warm summers and cold winters. The best wines from both varieties are found in the Côte d'Or and world-famous reds such as Gevrey-Chambertin, Vougeot and Nuits-St-Georges are found in the Côte de Nuits. Villages such as Volnay in the Côte de Beaune also produce some reds, but they are lighter and more elegant in style.

As is often the case in France, there is a 'quality pyramid' in place, from top to bottom:

- **Grand Cru:** e.g. Chambertin, Clos de la Roche, La Tâche and Échezeaux
- **Premier Cru:** e.g. Vosne-Romanée Premier Cru and Nuits-St-Georges Premier Cru
- **Village level:** e.g. Vosne-Romanée and Nuits-St-Georges
- **Regional:** Bourgogne Rouge (Red Burgundy)

Also found in

Pinot Noir is a challenge to grow primarily because of its thin skins, which makes it vulnerable to both rot and sunburn. It also prefers long, cooler growing seasons, so even though it is found throughout the vine-growing world, it thrives specifically in cool climate sites.

- **France:** elsewhere in France, Pinot Noir is the red grape of Sancerre in the Loire Valley and Alsace, and along with Pinot Meunier and Chardonnay, it's one of the major grapes that goes into champagne production. It is also found in Eastern France (in Savoie and Jura).
- **Germany:** here it is known as Spätburgunder and the main growing region is Baden but there are also plantings in **Italy** (where it is known as Pinot Nero), **Switzerland** and Eastern Europe, for example **Romania**.
- **England:** Pinot Noir is predominantly grown for sparkling wine production, although really promising still wines are increasingly being made from the variety.
- **United States:** in Oregon and California, especially in regions such as Sonoma and Carneros, prestigious bottles of Pinot are being made – as well as over the border in **Canada**.
- **New Zealand:** makes first-class wines, notably from Central Otago and Martinborough, with superlative bottles also coming from Marlborough, Nelson, Canterbury and Wairarapa.

- **Australia:** the cooler regions, such as Tasmania, the Yarra Valley, the Mornington Peninsula and Adelaide Hills, are also extremely suitable for Pinot Noir, as is Walker Bay in **South Africa** and the cooler regions of **Chile**.

Flavour profile

Pinot Noir berries are quite big with thin skins, which results in lighter coloured wines with softer tannins. In terms of flavour, think cranberry, raspberry and red cherry. Bigger, bolder Pinots can also display blue fruits such as blueberry along with spicy notes from oak maturation. While it has a reputation for being tricky to grow and make, it does express its terroir, or 'sense of place', well.

Food and occasions

Being light- to medium-bodied and with softer tannins, Pinot pairs brilliantly with duck, and game such as venison. It can also be enjoyed with chicken (try it with coq au vin), meatier fish (like tuna), as well as beetroot, mushrooms, truffles and a nut roast. It's also a classic variety to serve with turkey. To really understand the hype about this venerable grape variety, it's a good idea to spend a bit of money and so therefore it's very much a 'treat' bottle; one for busting out when you want to impress: date night, meet the parents, entertaining your boss, that sort of thing.

Affordability £–£££££

While the most expensive bottle (75cl) of wine ever sold was made from Pinot Noir, it isn't always that punchy price wise! Great value bottles can be found from as far afield as Chile to Romania and, even though the greatest bottles are indisputably Burgundian, I find the Southern Hemisphere provides fantastic value and is far easier to navigate, with New Zealand being my personal 'go to'.

Pinot Noir berries are
quite big with thin skins,
which results in lighter
coloured wines with
softer tannins:
in terms of flavour,
think cranberry,
raspberry and red cherry.

GRENACHE
(pronounced: Gren-ash)

Grenache (Noir) – or Garnacha – is actually a Spanish grape variety, but is arguably better known as Grenache, with many consequently assuming it is French; there are certainly more plantings in France than in Spain. As Garnacha, however, it can be a component of the Rioja blend – along with the primary varietal of Tempranillo – and it is also the bedrock of the wines from Priorat. Garnacha also makes wonderful, beautifully hued and berry-scented rosé from Navarra.

Also found in

Grenache is fairly widespread in southern France, where it can produce wines with quite high alcohol, but that are relatively light in colour, as demonstrated by the Grenache-based blends of the Côtes du Rhône; the southern Rhône being where the majority of French plantings can be found. Lower yielding and old bush vine Grenache are capable of producing wines with structure and longevity such as Châteauneuf-du-Pape, where Grenache can make up a significant portion of the blend. It is not typically found as a single varietal in the Rhône and is one of the grape varieties found in Gigondas, Vacqueyras, Côtes du Rhône Villages and the twenty communes that are allowed to append their name to it, such as Cairanne and Sablet. It is also grown in Provence and the Languedoc-Roussillon where, again, it is typically part of a red blend along with varieties such as Syrah, Mourvedre, Cinsault and Carignan.

Further afield, Grenache is also found in Sardinia (Italy), where it is known as Cannonau, and in the United States – the Californian Rhône Rangers and winemakers in Washington have enthusiastically adopted it. In Australia, it is a fundamental part of the GSM blends (Grenache, Syrah and Mourvèdre).

Flavour profile

Grenache is capable of producing quite an impressive range of wines from the deep rich, inky reds of Priorat to the juicier single varietal examples found in Australia, where the tannins are softer and the fruit profile errs towards red fruits rather than black, as it does in Côtes du Rhône wines, too.

Food and occasions

Pair with red meats (a classic roast beef or lamb) or rustic styles of food: slow-cooked casseroles and stews are superb as is a ratatouille or good old sausage and mash. Grenache is a great choice to pick at the pub or to enjoy with a cosy kitchen meal.

Affordability ££–£££

The juicy, fruity styles are way cheaper than the more structured examples, especially from sought-after places like Châteauneuf-du-Pape or Priorat.

DID YOU KNOW? Grenache used to be the world's second most planted grape variety but today languishes in seventh place behind other red grape varieties Cabernet Sauvignon, Merlot, Tempranillo and Syrah, and the whites Airén and Chardonnay.

NEBBIOLO
(pronounced: Neb-ee-oh-lo)

Nebbiolo (also known as Spanna) is Italy's most revered grape variety and is responsible for the wines of Barolo and Barbaresco. Both villages are located in the north of the country, in the Piedmont region, and the wines are capable of great longevity due to having both high acidity and firm tannins. Elsewhere in Piedmont, other wines are made from Nebbiolo that are both more affordable and easier to drink while a bit younger. These include wines labelled as Langhe Nebbiolo and Nebbiolo d'Alba, both DOC level wines, as opposed to the vaunted DOCG level that includes both Barolo and Barbaresco.

Also found in

Nebbiolo isn't widely planted outside Italy, although some very encouraging wines are coming out of Australia, especially from the state of Victoria, and California in the United States.

Flavour profile

Unusually for a wine with such firm tannins, Nebbiolo produces wines that are surprisingly light in colour. Its aromas and flavours are typically described as being like 'roses' and 'tar', along with raspberry and the ubiquitous red cherry that seems to be found in many Italian red wines.

WINE FACT The name of this variety is thought to come from the Italian word *nebbia*, meaning fog, which is frequently found in the vineyards in the autumn.

Food and occasions

Being pale in colour and quite structured, with high acidity, high tannins and those subtle fruit flavours, food wise, think game, pork, prosciutto, truffles and pasta dishes (pappardelle with braised beef shin is incredible), vegetarian pizza and hard cheeses. The wines are fairly 'cerebral' and really need to be drunk with food; these are NOT sofa or TV wines but bottles for cogitating over at the kitchen table while doing the crossword – while eating! They are also for your friends or family members who like something a little challenging.

Affordability £££

Pricey! Even the 'cheaper' bottles are likely to set you back over a tenner.

DID YOU KNOW? Nebbiolo is known for making quite lightly coloured wines despite having high tannins and acidity. This is because of the water-soluble pigments in its skins, resulting in a 'brick' colour as the colour compounds break down.

SANGIOVESE

(pronounced: San-gee-oh-vay-zee)

Sangiovese is the most widely planted red grape variety in Italy, especially in central Italy, where it is responsible for a fairly wide range of styles of red, from the juicy cherry-scented wines of basic Chianti – that famously used to be found in a little straw basket, or fiasco – to the denser, richer reds of Brunello di Montalcino.

The most popular or notable wines made from Sangiovese are:
- **Chianti DOCG:** there are eight subzones that can use the name and Sangiovese must make up no more than 70 per cent of the blend
- **Chianti Classico DOCG:** identified not only by name but by a black rooster on the bottom of the neck foil
- **Chianti Classico Riserva:** has to have twenty-four months of oak ageing
- **Chianti Gran Selezione:** for the very best wines, with a minimum ageing of thirty months

Brunello di Montalcino DOCG is also Tuscan, more specifically from Siena, and is made from 100 per cent Sangiovese, with the wines having to be aged in oak for at least two years. The wines can only be released on to the market after five years of total ageing, six for the Riserva wines.

Rosso di Montalcino DOC also produces single varietal Sangiovese wines but they are released onto the market earlier and so are less serious in style.

Vino Nobile di Montepulciano DOCG is blended with other varieties such as Canaiolo and is aged for two years, or three for a riserva.

For Carmignano DOCG, Sangiovese must make up at least 50 per cent of the blend.

Also found in

Fine examples of Sangiovese are coming out of North and South America and also Australia, especially from the King Valley and McLaren Vale.

Flavour profile

Alongside notes of cherry are those of herbs and tea, as well as spicy notes if oak has been used and a slight savoury edge. Tannins are lower than in wines made from Nebbiolo but acidity is brisk, as is often the case with Italian reds, and wines can range from light- to full-bodied, although its natural style is on the lighter side. Colour wise it's most definitely on the lighter side too.

Food and occasions

Sangiovese – certainly Chianti – is very much your 'go-to' wine for tomato-based pizza and pasta: as our favourite mantra advises: 'what grows together goes together'! Charcuterie is also a very sound choice, as is a lentil stew (with or without bacon or sausages). Usually juicy and fairly fruity with cherry notes, the entry-level wines can be uncomplicated – there's no need to sip or savour these – so they're wonderful wines for relaxing with during the week.

Affordability ££

Some Chianti can be as cheap as chips, but if you spend a bit more you'll be able to appreciate the grace yet power of this variety.

WINTER FOOD AND WINE MATCHING

Winter is all about comfort, and comfort definitely means carbs! I'm not fussy when it comes to this sensational seasonal tummy filler and am as likely to cook with rice as with pasta or potato. To add extra texture and richness, I reach for cream or coconut milk. With energy bills still alarmingly high, it's nice to warm up with a plate of steaming food and to pile on an extra jumper, slipper socks AND slippers.

There are still a lot of seasonal veggies on the scene in winter – beetroot, cauliflower, Brussels sprouts and parsnips – and they are surprisingly versatile, equally tasty in curries, savoury tarts or simply roasted in the oven. Vegetables have the huge advantage of being not only healthy but also cheap, and even simple dishes can taste delicious and be on the table in no time at all. For winter there are two veg-packed recipes that are slightly spicy – a harissa-roasted seasonal veggies with salmon and a cauliflower curry. Both are ideal with an off-dry white such as a Riesling or an ultra aromatic Gewürztraminer. Two game-based meals – duck and venison – complete the recipes and although these two require a bit more input time wise they are a total treat for the taste buds; they're my go-to dinner-party dishes for the festive season.

What's in season in the winter?

HERBS

chervil, parsley, thyme

SALADS

chicory, radicchio, watercress

GREEN VEGGIES

Brussels sprouts, cabbage, celery,
kale, leeks, spinach

OTHER VEGGIES

beetroot, carrots, cauliflower,
celeriac, Jerusalem artichokes,
mushrooms, onions, parsnips,
potatoes, pumpkin, purple sprouting
broccoli, red cabbage, shallots,
spring onion, swede, sweet potato,
turnips, wild mushrooms

FRUIT AND NUTS

apples, blood oranges, chestnuts,
clementines, cranberries, pears,
pomegranate, quince, rhubarb

FISH AND SEAFOOD

clams, cod, crab, cuttlefish, hake,
lobster, monkfish, mussels, oysters,
plaice, pollack, prawns, sardines,
scallop, seabass, skate, squid

MEAT

beef, chicken, duck, goose, grouse,
guinea fowl, hare, lamb, partridge,
pheasant, pork, quail, rabbit, turkey,
venison

FOOD TYPE	BEST WINE TYPES: Exotic Fruits & Spice, Blackberries & Spice and Red Fruits & Roses
Herbs:	off-dry Riesling
Salads:	off-dry Riesling, Torrontés
Green veggies:	Grenache, Sangiovese
Other veggies:	Gewürztraminer, Grenache, Malbec, Nebbiolo, off-dry Riesling, Pinotage, Pinot Gris, Pinot Noir, Syrah, Torrontés
Fish/seafood:	Gewürztraminer, Muscat, off-dry Riesling, Pinot Gris, Pinot Noir, Torrontés
Meat:	Gewürztraminer, Grenache, Malbec, Nebbiolo, Pinot Gris, Pinot Noir, Pinotage, Sangiovese, Syrah, Zinfandel

WINTER RECIPES

Beetroot-marinated Salmon with Harissa-roasted
Winter Veggies and Feta – 246

—

Duck Breast with Red Cabbage and Potato
Dauphinoise – 248

—

Cauliflower, Chickpea and Coconut Curry
with Baby Spinach – 250

—

Mini Venison Wellingtons with Parsnip Purée
and Steamed Sprouts – 251

BEETROOT-MARINATED SALMON WITH HARISSA-ROASTED WINTER VEGGIES AND FETA

You need to marinate the salmon for 45 minutes before cooking, so make sure you leave yourself enough time. It's worth it though, as the result is a vibrantly coloured winter meal that makes use of the wonderful abundance of seasonal root veggies. For a vegetarian option, serve without the salmon; for a vegan dish, roast the harissa-coated winter vegetables on their own without the fish or cheese.

+ **WINE** A subtly scented, lightly floral Torrontés would be a terrific match here or an off-dry Riesling, as the subtle sweetness will temper the heat of the harissa. If you fancy a red, a supple, ripe, warm-climate Pinot Noir would be robust enough to cope with the flavours and have enough fruit ripeness for the spice. Pinot Noir and beetroot also match well. For something a bit different, try a single varietal, juicy Australian Grenache.

SERVES 4

For the fish and marinade
4x salmon fillets, skin on
2x beetroot bulbs, peeled and grated
2x tbsp creamed horseradish, from a jar
2x tbsp olive oil
2x tsp Dijon mustard
1x handful fresh dill, chopped
1x juice of a lemon

For the veggies:
2x red onions, peeled and cut into chunks
300gm parsnips, peeled and cut into thick matchsticks
4x beetroot bulbs, peeled and cut into chunks
400gm rainbow carrots, tops cut off and peeled but leave whole
1x 200gm packet of Feta, cut into small cubes
2x tbsp harissa paste (less if you are not so keen on spice)
A good glug of olive oil

For the horseradish cream:
1x 200ml crème fraîche
1x tbsp creamed horseradish, from a jar
1x lemon – zest and juice

Put the salmon fillets, skin side down, into a small roasting tin. Combine the marinade ingredients in a bowl, reserving a tablespoon of chopped dill to sprinkle on the finished dish, then spoon the marinade evenly over the salmon fillets and pop in the fridge for 45 minutes.

Meanwhile, preheat your oven to 200/180°C fan and prepare your vegetables for roasting. Once they're peeled and chopped, put them all into a roasting tin along with the cubed feta, add the harissa, a liberal glug of olive oil and mix well. Roast for half an hour, shaking or turning them a couple of times so they cook evenly.

Make the horseradish cream: combine the crème fraiche, horseradish, lemon zest and juice and give a good stir.

When the veggies have been in the oven for 30 minutes, take the salmon out of the fridge, remove the marinade (simply scrape it off each fillet) and place the fish (which should now be a lovely colour from the beetroot marinade) into the oven for 10–12 minutes, checking with a knife to make sure that it is cooked.

Once both the roasted vegetables and the fish are ready, remove from the oven and place the vegetables and feta into four warmed dinner bowls with the fish nestled on top. Sprinkle with the reserved dill and serve the horseradish cream on the side.

DUCK BREAST WITH RED CABBAGE AND POTATO DAUPHINOISE

Duck breast can be a real treat in the winter and this indulgent dish is a firm favourite in our household. It also has the added advantage that it is always cooked by my husband!

+ WINE Any red berry fruited wine from the Red Fruits & Roses branch of the Tree would be a fantastic match with both the duck and the rich potatoes. The red fruits work well with the meat (red cherries and duck are a winning combination) but acidity is also needed to cut through the richness. For these reasons Barolo or Barbaresco (the Nebbiolo grape) is a classic match, as is a Pinot Noir – my personal preference would always be for the softer Pinot, though Sangiovese and Grenache would also suit.

SERVES 4

4x duck breasts

For the red cabbage
1x head of red
   cabbage, sliced
200ml malt vinegar
125g golden caster sugar
125g melted butter
Salt and pepper

For the potato dauphinoise:
50g butter
3x cloves garlic, finely
   sliced
1x 50g tin of anchovies,
   drained and chopped
500ml double cream
90g Parmesan, grated
1kg potatoes

Place the sliced red cabbage in a heavy saucepan along with the vinegar, sugar and butter. Season with salt and pepper, stir well and place on a low to medium heat, covered for 30 minutes and then uncovered for a further 30–45 minutes, stirring regularly; it can take quite a long time!

Score the duck breasts diagonally across the skin with a sharp knife every 1.5 cm and set aside at room temperature for 30 minutes, covering with a sheet or two of kitchen roll to absorb any juice.

Now make the potato dauphinoise. Preheat the oven to 220/200°C fan. Heat the butter in a large frying pan and fry the garlic and anchovies on a low temperature for around 5 minutes before adding the double cream. Turn up the heat and simmer until bubbling, switch off the heat and then add in the Parmesan cheese so that it melts. Slice the potatoes into 3mm slices (using a food processor, mandolin or by hand) and then cover the bottom of an earthenware dish with a layer of potato, before spooning over half the creamy mixture, then another layer of potatoes and another layer of mixture. Put foil on top and place in the oven for 45 minutes. Check the potatoes are soft and ready with a sharp knife.

To cook the duck, put the breasts in a frying pan skin side down on a low heat for 15–20 minutes to get the fat out. Then turn them over, increasing the heat slightly to medium for a further 8–10 minutes, turning occasionally if the underside is starting to get too hot. Cook for longer if you like your breasts well done. Remove from the heat, cover with foil and allow to rest for 15–20 minutes – this is crucial to make sure that the breasts are super soft and tender. Serve on warmed plates along with the potato and red cabbage.

CAULIFLOWER, CHICKPEA AND COCONUT CURRY WITH BABY SPINACH

There's nothing like a warming, lightly spiced curry on a winter's evening, and this dish uses one of my favourite vegetables – cauliflower – which is fantastic in curries, soups, as a cauliflower cheese or simply roasted with other seasonal vegetables.

+ WINE Gewürztraminer is a great match both with ginger and with coconut, so it's an ideal wine for this dish. In fact, a lot of wines with a suggestion of sweetness would work well as it helps the wine to cope brilliantly with the spicy flavours. Other aromatic white varieties with a touch of residual sugar would be good too, such as a Muscat or an off-dry Riesling.

SERVES 4

3x tbsp olive oil
1x onion, finely chopped
2 cloves garlic, finely sliced
3–4cm piece of ginger, peeled and finely grated
1 large cauliflower cut into small florets
1x tbsp Madras curry power
1x tsp ground turmeric
1x tsp ground cumin
2x tsp black mustard seeds
400g tin of full-fat coconut milk
400g chickpeas, drained and rinsed
240g baby spinach
Salt and pepper
1 large handful of coriander, chopped for garnish

Heat the oil in a large saucepan and fry the onions, garlic and ginger for around 10 minutes.

While they are softening, steam the cauliflower florets – the longer they steam for, the less cooking time is required later; I'd recommend 5 minutes – then set aside.

Add the spices and mustard seeds to the onion mix, stirring well. Then add in the coconut milk, cauliflower and drained chickpeas, season and simmer on a low heat until the cauliflower is cooked – this will take a further 8–10 minutes depending on the size of the florets. Check to see if they are are done using a sharp knife. A few minutes before the dish is ready, add the baby spinach leaves and wilt.

Season and garnish with the chopped coriander and serve – I love this with basmati rice, pilau rice and/or a naan.

250

MINI VENISON WELLINGTONS WITH PARSNIP PURÉE AND STEAMED SPROUTS

One of my favourite ever dishes – a bit time consuming but a real showstopper and guaranteed to impress at a dinner party! It would make a fabulous alternative to a traditional Christmas Day lunch too.

+ WINE As venison is a lean meat, wine wise there are a number of different options that would be lip-smacking!. Like duck, venison works particularly well with Pinot Noir and Nebbiolo – both from the Red Fruits & Roses branch of the Tree – but a peppery Syrah would also be absolutely divine and ultimately gets my vote. Alternatively for something a bit richer and riper and with a nod to the port-rich sauce, a full-throttled Pinotage with plenty of dark berry fruits would be terrific.

SERVES 6

For the 2x mini venison Wellingtons:
700–800g venison loin
1x tbsp olive oil
1.5x tbsp English mustard
50g butter
2x small shallots, finely chopped
1x clove garlic, crushed
500g chestnut mushrooms, very, very finely chopped (use a food processor)
1 tbsp thyme leaves, finely chopped
12–16 slices prosciutto
Plain flour
375g pack all-butter puff pastry
2 egg yolks, beaten

For the sauce:
25g butter
1x onion, finely chopped
3x sprigs thyme
1x tsp plain flour
25ml Late Bottled Vintage (LBV) port
12x peppercorns
1x tbsp red wine vinegar

For the parsnip purée:
1kg parsnips, peeled and chopped into equal size pieces
2x cloves of garlic, peeled but whole
50g butter
150ml double cream

1x 750g bag Brussels sprouts, trimmed

For the mini venison Wellingtons:
Pat the loin dry to absorb any juices then cut in two equal pieces. Season each half with salt and pepper, heat the olive oil in a frying pan and sear each loin for around 7 minutes, until nicely browned. Brush with the mustard (about 2x tsp per fillet), then set aside to cool before transferring to the fridge to chill for a further 30 minutes.

Clean the frying pan, melt the butter and cook the shallots and garlic until soft. Add the finely chopped mushrooms, thyme and a pinch of salt and cook for around 10–12 minutes, until it has a paste-like consistency and the water from the mushrooms has evaporated. Allow to cool.

Lay two pieces of clingfilm out on a flat surface – one piece per fillet. Each piece needs to be big enough to roll up each fillet once covered with prosciutto slices (see below) and the mushroom mix. Place 6–8 slices of prosciutto on each bit of clingfilm horizontally, ensuring that the slices overlap. Spoon the mushroom mix in a thin layer over the bottom of the prosciutto slices and then place each venison fillet on top, in the middle of the mushrooms, before carefully wrapping the prosciutto and mushroom around the fillet, using the edge of the clingfilm to help. Tighten the ends to secure, and then chill for around half an hour.

Cut the puff pastry in half and roll each half out onto a lightly floured chopping board – you will need to do this one at a time. Roll out enough pastry to make sure that the sheet is big enough to completely encase each venison half. Brush the top ¼ of the rolled-out pastry with the beaten egg yolk – this will help the parcel seal. The covered fillet can now be taken out of the clingfilm case and placed in the middle of the pastry. Roll the pastry over the fillet, making a secure parcel. Close up the ends as neatly as you can, using more egg yolk to help. Finally, brush the outside with beaten egg yolk too then repeat the process with the second fillet.

Chill for at least half an hour, although it can be chilled for up to 24 hours. Preheat the oven to 220/200°C fan, oil a baking sheet and gently score the pastry every ½ inch or so, so that the pastry won't get soggy. Put the mini Wellingtons onto the sheet and cook for around 25 minutes, making sure that the pastry is golden. Remove from the oven and allow to rest for around 20 minutes. It is then ready to be sliced and served.

For the sauce:

Melt the butter in a saucepan or frying pan and add the finely chopped onion and the thyme for around 10 minutes or until the onion is soft. Add the flour for 1 minute and then the port, peppercorns and the red wine vinegar, cooking to reduce by about ⅔. Pass through a sieve prior to serving.

For the parsnip purée:

Bring a pan of salted water to the boil. Add the parsnip pieces and the whole garlic cloves and boil until the parsnips are soft – check with a knife at around 8 minutes. Drain, add the butter and cream and blitz in a food processor until smooth.

Brussels sprouts:

Trim the sprouts and steam until cooked, around six minutes.

To serve:

Spoon the parsnip purée onto warmed plates with a slice (or two) of venison Wellington on top, drizzling some port sauce over the meat. Serve the sprouts in a bowl or on the side of the plate.

OTHER WINTER WINE STYLES

Fortified and Sweet Wines

At no other time during the course of the year do I reach for a fortified or sweet wine as much as I do in the winter – or, to be precise, at Christmas. Groaning cheese boards go hand in hand with port – or other sweet wines such as a Hungarian Tokaji – and certain styles of sherry and sweet wines are an epic match with mince pies, Christmas cake and, of course, Christmas pud.

Lighter styles are also extremely refreshing throughout the year (think fino sherry), while less unctuous, more vibrant, lemon- and honey-scented pudding wines are perfection with summer fruits and meringue. Chocolate is a surprisingly tricky match but there's pretty much a wine for every sweet treat. The only rule to follow when matching sweet wines with sweet food is that the wine has to be sweeter than the food, otherwise what's in your glass may seem bitter or astringent.

Fortified Wines

These are wines that have been 'fortified' or strengthened by the addition of alcohol – usually brandy or a neutral grape spirit – to increase the alcoholic strength. The main styles of fortified wines include sherry, port, Madeira, Vin Doux Naturel (VDN) wines and Rutherglen Muscats.

Sherry

Sherries are Spanish fortified wines that can range from intensely dry and tangy to the richest, sweetest pudding wines, best poured over ice cream. The main sherry grape is Palomino, which is grown on the brilliant-white albariza soils of Jerez in Andalucía, southern Spain.

All sherries essentially fit into one of two different categories:

- **Fino:** lighter, dry styles of 'biological' sherry, where a film of yeast called flor has been allowed to develop
- **Oloroso:** dry sherries where the growth of flor did not occur

After the harvest and fermentation, the wine is fortified with grape spirit and, crucially, the degree of fortification determines which style of sherry the wine is to become; flor can't survive in alcohols of over about 16 per cent. Therefore, if a fino style of sherry is desired, fortification will be around 15–15.5 per cent, but for the richer oloroso wines, fortification is more likely to be around 18 per cent.

The key to the fino styles of wine is the development of this essential flor, which develops naturally on top of the sherry in the barrels or butts. The sherry needs to be regularly refreshed with younger wine, in order to provide the yeast with the nutrients it would otherwise use up. It is this need to refresh the wine that is the principle behind the 'solera system': essentially 'topping up' the wine to keep the yeasts happy and active but with the added benefit of blending the wines too. The solera system therefore is an ingenious and complex process of fractional blending, also known as 'running the scales'.

Below are the key styles of sherry:

- **Manzanilla:** essentially a fino but with the bodega or sherry house being located in Sanlúcar de Barrameda rather than Jerez. The wines are lighter, tangier and saltier in style, being closer to the coast
- **Fino:** a dry, light, elegant sherry aged in Jerez under a layer of flor
- **Amontillado:** a fino sherry that loses its layer of flor and as a result of this contact with the air (flor prevents oxidation) becomes slightly darker in colour and a bit nuttier
- **Palo Cortado:** a bit of a rarity, this is a sherry that started life as a fino or amontillado but lost its flor and as a result, stylistically is a sort of hybrid between a fino/amontillado and an oloroso
- **Oloroso:** fortified to 18 per cent, these sherries are made without flor and are browner and more concentrated, with notes of nuts and citrus peel
- **Pale cream:** a sweetened biological sherry
- **Cream sherry:** an oloroso sherry sweetened with Pedro Ximénez wine
- **PX:** an intensely sweet, raisined dessert wine made from Pedro Ximénez grapes

TIP Becoming increasingly fashionable and remaining extraordinarily good value, sherry is an exciting category to watch.

Port

Port is, unsurprisingly, from Portugal, specifically from the beautiful town of Oporto. Like sherry, port is an Iberian fortified wine that is steeped in centuries-old tradition. Many of the most famous and renowned port houses – or quintas – are owned by English families (such as Warre's, Dow's, Taylor's and Graham's) and perhaps it is this long-held association with the United Kingdom, gentlemen's clubs, passing the port to the left and the cheese board that makes port feel so rarefied, exclusive and a bit old-fashioned. However, many of the houses are forward thinking too, even while embracing the traditions of the past, and now produce exceptional still (especially red) wines. Pink port has also been introduced into the market and houses are also promoting white port and tonic as a delicious alternative to gin.

Sherry and port are both made in a range of styles but sherry is especially fêted for its elegance and restraint, with the lighter wines such as manzanilla and fino making wonderful apéritifs that are best drunk while they are young and fresh. Port is quite the opposite, with the more illustrious styles being deep in colour, fully flavoured, capable of great longevity and complexity and enjoyed as a digestif at the end of a meal. Vintage port is the very essence of this and arguably the heartbeat of the industry, made in tiny quantities but creating the halo effect for the other types of wine that are produced.

Port is made from a number of different black grape varieties – notably Touriga Nacional, Tinta Barroca, Touriga Franca, Tinta Roriz (Tempranillo) and Tinta Cão – grown on staggeringly steep terraced vineyards that require picking by hand. Once the grapes are picked and crushed, it is essential to extract the colour and tannins as quickly as possible, as the fortifying spirit is added after just a few days. The high level of alcohol (77 per cent) in the spirit kills the yeast, which therefore causes the fermentation to stop, and because the spirit is added before all of the sugar has been fermented into alcohol, the resulting wine is sweet with an alcohol level of around 19–20 per cent.

Historically the grapes were trodden by foot in lagares to extract the all-important colour and tannin without too much bitterness, though this practice has long since been modernised. Once the port is made, it is usually shipped down the river to the lodges at Vila Nova de Gaia for ageing. There are two main ways of ageing port, in bottle – bottle-aged – and in barrel – barrel-aged.

BOTTLE-AGED PORT

Vintage port is made from one specific single vintage that has been 'declared' (by the port house) when the quality is deemed exceptional. Aged in wood for a minimum of two years – often three – the wine is then bottled without filtration and can age for years in the bottle, improving over many decades and throwing a significant sediment. It is this sediment that requires vintage port to be decanted.

Single-Quinta vintage ports are similar to vintage ports but tend to be made from a single estate and from a single vintage, usually made in undeclared years.

Late Bottled Vintage (LBV) port is a vintage port that has been aged for four to six years in cask and then bottled. They are intended to be drunk earlier than vintage port and are generally made in undeclared years. Some are also bottled without filtration so require decanting while others are fined and often filtered, which results in no sediment and negates the need for decanting. Crusted ports are essentially the same thing as traditional, unfiltered LBVs, in that they throw a crust or sediment and are intended to emulate the character of vintage port but at a cheaper price.

Ruby port is one of the simplest styles of port, aged for around two to three years before it is bottled, and boasts charming upfruit flavours. A Reserve Ruby is more premium.

Sherry and port are both made in a range of styles but sherry is especially fêted for its elegance and restraint, with the lighter wines such as manzanilla and fino making wonderful apéritifs that are best drunk while they are young and fresh. Port is quite the opposite, with the more illustrious styles being deep in colour, fully flavoured, capable of great longevity and complexity and enjoyed as a digestif at the end of a meal.

Barrel-aged ports – as the name suggests – age in cask and are ready to drink once in bottle, with no need for decanting. The extended time in wood not only softens the liquid but also has a marked impact on the colour and these fortified wines are known as tawny ports.

Entry-level tawny port isn't actually aged for very long in wood at all to reach that beautiful tawny hue, but instead is made to appear lighter by using less premium grapes from less premium regions or by blending in white port.

Aged tawny on the other hand is more premium and the label on the bottle clearly indicates how long it has been aged for at the lodges in Vila Nova de Gaia, with the designations being 10, 20, 30 and Over 40 years old. The wines are made from high-quality ports made in undeclared years and like vintage ports, are sensational with cheese. Like the lighter styles of sherry, tawny port can also be drunk chilled as an apéritif.

Colheitas are also tawny ports but made from a single year and aged for a minimum of seven years. Like aged tawny port, the date of bottling is found on the label and as these are barrel- rather than bottle-aged wines, they should be enjoyed within a year or two of that date.

Madeira

Named after the Portuguese island where it is made, Madeira is probably the most 'under the radar' of all fortified wines, even though it is capable of making wines of quite extraordinary longevity. Centuries ago, it was discovered that the wines tasted better once they had been transported across the sea, baking under the sun, and so now this effect is mimicked on the island using a process called the 'estufa system'.

Wines made using the estufa process tend to be cheaper, bulk wines such as Three Year Old or Five Year Old Reserve wines. The premium wines are made by a natural, gentle process which leaves the wine stored in pipes in the building's eaves to be heated by the sun; this can take decades.

The four grape varieties that can make varietal Madeira are Sercial, Verdelho, Bual and Malmsey, with Sercial being the driest and most acidic and Malmsey the richest and sweetest. The most common term found on a label for these wines is Ten Year Old Special Reserve, with the premium being Vintage (or frasqueira) Madeira.

Vin Doux Naturel and Rutherglen Muscats

These two styles of fortified wine straddle pudding wines and fortified wines as they are both sweet and fortified, rather like PX sherry.

Like port, French Vin Doux Naturel (VDN) wines have their fermentation arrested through the addition of a spirit, with the resulting wines being both sweet and quite alcoholic – around 15–18 per cent. Common grapes include Muscat – such as Muscat de Beaumes de Venise and Muscat de Rivesaltes – or Grenache, which makes VDNs from the appellations of Rasteau, Maury (an amazing match with chocolate) and Banyuls.

Over on the other side of the world, in Victoria, Australia, and the region of Rutherglen specifically, the most delicious fortified Muscats are also made. While the French Muscat-based Beaumes de Venise and Rivesaltes tend to be golden in colour and quite delicate and grapey, these ones pack a serious flavour punch and are incredibly sweet and unctuous, with notes of figs, Christmas cake, prunes, raisins and stewed fruits. The grape used is brown Muscat – a type of Muscat Blanc à Petits Grains – and they are left in the vineyard until really ripe and on their way to resembling raisins before they are picked. Like port, they undergo only a brief fermentation before it is arrested with grape spirit. The resulting wine – which is very sweet and quite high in alcohol – is then aged in wooden casks. There are four different quality levels of this Muscat: Rutherglen Muscat, Classic, Grand and then Rare. Rutherglen Muscat is my preferred Christmas pudding wine match as it literally tastes like Christmas pudding in a glass . . . it's definitely following the complement rather than contrast food and wine matching route!

Sweet Wines

The best sweet wines are among the trickiest types of wine to make, and are like vinous jewels with their rich golden colours and sumptuous fruits.

Botrytis wines

Botrytis cinerea, aka 'noble rot', is actually a desired rot, as opposed to the dreaded grey rot that can decimate a harvest. Specific climatic conditions are required for its growth – principally fog followed by sunshine, which keeps the development of the rot in check. Spores of this benevolent rot develop on the grapes and essentially shrivel them, without imparting any notes of mould, concentrating the sugars inside to create extremely sweet grapes. Many superlative styles of botrytis pudding wine are made, but the most famous example is Sauternes.

Solely a sweet wine appellation in the region of Graves, Bordeaux, Sauternes is made of a blend of three different grape varieties – Sémillon, Sauvignon Blanc and Muscadelle – with Sémillon accounting for the principal component of the blend. Fermentation usually happens in oak – with a proportion often being new – with maturation in oak following afterwards, adding notes of spice to the sweet fruit. The resulting wine often tastes of orange peel, honey blossom, acacia, marmalade, citrus and spice, and is exquisite with strawberries, crème brûlée or lighter citrus-based puddings such as tarts. The very best wines are classified as either first or second growths, although the exceptional Château Yquem is a stand-alone Premier Cru Supérieur.

This marvellous, transformative rot is also responsible for the world-class Tokaji from Hungary. Here the principal grapes are Furmint and Hárslevelü, and although there are a few different styles of this sweet wine, the principal one is Aszú. The botrytised grapes are hand-picked and fermented, with barrel maturation lending an oxidative character to the wines. With a beautiful amber colour and delicious notes of marmalade and apricot, Tokaji is sensational with blue cheese, Christmas pudding and chocolate-orange desserts. The 'Puttonyos' on the label tells the consumer how sweet the wine is: the higher the number the sweeter the wine, so 6 puttonyos is sweeter than 5.

Many of the best sweet wines in the world come from Germany and Austria and are often made from the Riesling grape, as the naturally high levels of acidity balance beautifully with the sweetness of the wines. The sweetest of these, and those that are nearly always affected by noble rot, are Auslese, Beerenauslese and Trockenbeerenauslese (TBA). These wines are typically quite low in alcohol as they are too sweet for all of the sugar to ferment.

In France, outside of Sauternes, sweet botrytised wines are made in Alsace from Pinot Gris, Riesling, Gewürztraminer and Muscat, in a category called Sélection des Grains Nobles (SGN). In the Loire Valley, excellent sweet wines made from the Chenin Blanc grape are also usually affected by botrytis such as Bonnezeaux and Quarts de Chaume.

There are also many excellent sweet wines made outside of Europe from botrytised grapes, in countries such as Australia, New Zealand, the United States and South Africa.

Eiswein or icewine

Another extraordinary way to make sweet wines is to allow the grapes to freeze on the vine. Again, this requires very specific climatic conditions – notably cold, marginal climates – and the two most renowned countries for Eiswein or Icewine production are Germany and Canada, though Austria does make tiny quantities.

The grapes stay on the vine until the very end of autumn or the beginning of winter, and as the temperature drops, ice forms on the berries. This serves to concentrate the sugars in the berries – as well as the acidity – which are then picked by hand while they are still frozen. The wines are not affected by botrytis.

Icewine is frequently made from the Vidal grape, which is a French hybrid, as well as the red grape Cabernet Franc and better known varieties such as Riesling. German (and Austrian) Eiswein is typically made from Riesling.

Straw wines

Another way of producing sweet wines is to dry the grapes on straw mats, which encourages them to shrivel up and become slightly raisined. This is called vin de paille in France and strohwein in Germany, although some of the best known examples are actually Italian – notably Vin Santo and Recioto della Valpolicella.

Vin Santo is from the region of Tuscany and is made from the Trebbiano and Malvasia grapes, dried on straw mats and then aged in barrel for at least three years, usually longer. Oxidation results in a deep amber hue and they often have a 'rancio' aroma and flavour, which is best described as nutty.

Recioto della Valpolicella is made principally from the same Corvina grape that goes into Valpolicella, which, rather unusually for a sweet wine, is red. The grapes are left to raisin in designated drying rooms, resulting in a sweet red wine with distinct notes of red and black cherry that make it a great match with chocolate or Black Forest gâteau. Amarone is also made from dried grapes but it is dry or just off-dry rather than being sweet.

Late harvest wines

One of the simplest ways of making a sweet wine is to leave the grapes on the vine for longer, so that the fruit becomes riper and the sugars more concentrated. An example of this would be a Vendage Tardive or 'late harvest' sweet wine from Alsace. Excellent examples are also made in the Southern Hemisphere, especially in South Africa from the Muscat de Frontignan grape.

Sparkling

The vast majority of sparkling wines are dry (Brut) or just off-dry, but sweeter styles such as Demi-Sec (medium dry) and Doux (sweet) are fabulous with fruit-based puddings. They may be rather rare, but sparkling Icewines are also extraordinary. And expensive!

Another really wonderful, delicate, subtly sweet and subtly sparkling wine is made from the Moscato – or Muscat – grape. Moscato d'Asti is from the Piedmont region of Italy, and is low in alcohol and froth, but high in flavour and general deliciousness. Rather than being renowned as a pudding wine however, it is often cited as being the best breakfast or hangover wine!

REMEMBER Asti Spumante and Moscato d'Asti are both made from the Moscato grape and both come from Asti, but Moscato d'Asti is superior in quality and therefore more expensive.

Lambrusco is another sweet, sparkling Italian wine – from Central Italy – and is made from the red grape variety of the same name.

Matching by Food Category

Remember, the golden rules are to
match the weight of the wine to the
weight of the food, what grows together
and flavour balancing. Also think about
how the food has been prepared and
watch out for any tricky sauces, spices or
ingredients. These techniques can then
be taken a step further and applied
to specific food categories – such
as poultry, fish, red meat, vegetables,
cheese and puddings.

PAIRING WINE WITH EVERY FOOD

Poultry

Poultry actually encompasses quite a wide range of different seasonal birds, from the perennially popular chicken through to duck, goose and of course turkey – which is very much associated with festive fare. Because the birds vary both in their seasonality and flavour intensity, they suit different colours and styles of wines throughout the year, predominantly ranging from whites (especially Chardonnay) to lighter reds. In addition to considering the type of bird, seasoning and sauces also play a critical role – poultry dishes are cooked and served in a plethora of ways. So, try to decide what flavour stands out the most; is it coming from the sauce or spices rather than the bird itself? This will very much determine what style of wine to select, from a crisp white for a chicken Caesar salad in the summer to a red with roast turkey and all the trimmings on Christmas Day.

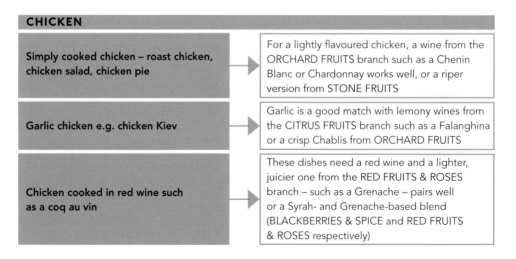

CHICKEN

Simply cooked chicken – roast chicken, chicken salad, chicken pie	For a lightly flavoured chicken, a wine from the ORCHARD FRUITS branch such as a Chenin Blanc or Chardonnay works well, or a riper version from STONE FRUITS
Garlic chicken e.g. chicken Kiev	Garlic is a good match with lemony wines from the CITRUS FRUITS branch such as a Falanghina or a crisp Chablis from ORCHARD FRUITS
Chicken cooked in red wine such as a coq au vin	These dishes need a red wine and a lighter, juicier one from the RED FRUITS & ROSES branch – such as a Grenache – pairs well or a Syrah- and Grenache-based blend (BLACKBERRIES & SPICE and RED FRUITS & ROSES respectively)

Chicken casserole	A richer casserole with a tomato base needs a slightly more structured red such as a Chianti (from Sangiovese) from RED FRUITS & ROSES or a Merlot from BERRIES & CHOCOLATE
Spicy chicken dishes: Indian or Thai curry	For tomato-based chicken curries, try a ripe, full red with soft tannins from BLACKBERRIES & SPICE whilst a coconut-based Thai benefits from an aromatic off-dry white such as Riesling, Pinot Gris or Gewürztraminer: EXOTIC FRUITS & SPICE

TURKEY

Roast turkey and all the trimmings	If serving white, then you need a full-bodied variety such as Chardonnay from STONE FRUITS but for reds, a lighter red such as a Pinot Noir (or a riper, warm climate wine) from RED FRUIT & ROSES is a classic choice, though I love a Syrah (BLACKBERRIES & SPICE) or a Rioja – BERRIES & CHOCOLATE
Turkey escalope or schnitzel	Again, Pinot Noir from RED FRUIT & ROSES gets top spot but if you are looking for a white, try a ripe Chardonnay from STONE FRUITS
Turkey pie, turkey curry or turkey risotto	A turkey pie loves Chardonnay (STONE FRUITS), a curry favours a ripe red such as a soft Malbec from BLACKBERRIES & SPICE or an aromatic white from EXOTIC FRUITS & SPICE. For turkey risotto, a light red with restrained flavours but good acidity is ideal – an Italian such as a Dolcetto (SOFT & JUICY) or Barbera (BERRIES & CHOCOLATE)

GOOSE

Roast goose	A cherry-scented wine! Think Pinot Noir or Nebbiolo from RED FRUITS & ROSES

DUCK

Roast duck, duck pancakes, duck breast	The RED FRUITS & ROSES branch is ideal: fresh acidity to cut through the fat

Fish & Seafood

When it comes to fish and seafood, it is a good idea to pretty much take red wine off the table. The tannins can make fish taste slightly metallic and any medium- to full-bodied examples would overwhelm the flavours and structure of most fish dishes. Therefore, fish and seafood should predominantly be matched with white or rosé wines. The only exception would be meatier fish such as tuna, which can pair very nicely with light and fruity reds with low tannins that can even be served chilled in the summer months. Once you've considered the weight of the fish, the second key consideration is the overall flavour. Many dishes are served with little or no sauce – perhaps just a drizzle of olive oil and lemon – and thus suit subtle, crisp whites, while dishes with richer sauces such as Marie Rose and thermidor require a riper, fuller-bodied white to match.

Oysters	A crisp delicate white such as a Chablis from the ORCHARD FRUITS branch or a Muscadet from the Loire Valley
Sushi	Champagne: a fabulous match!
Delicate white fish with lemon and olive oil	A light, lemony, citrus-scented wine from the CITRUS FRUITS branch such as a Falanghina or Grüner Veltliner or from ORCHARD FRUITS – a delicate Pinot Grigio for example
Shellfish, including prawns, lobster and scallops	Fresh whites from the ORCHARD FRUITS or CITRUS FRUITS branches or rosés are also fabulous with squid, paella and Provençal Bouillabaisse fish stew
Seafood in richer sauces such as Marie Rose or thermidor	A textured, medium- to full-bodied white such as a Chardonnay or Albariño from STONE FRUITS
Fish cakes or fish served with a parsley or tarragon sauce	To match the herbal flavours, try a white from the GREEN FRUITS & GRASS branch such as a Sauvignon Blanc or Vermentino
Meatier fish such as fish pie, monkfish, turbot or salmon	Here the best bet is to go down the 'complement' route and so something from the STONE FRUITS branch would be great, from a Chardonnay to a Fiano or Albariño
Grilled or pan-fried tuna	Pretty much the only fish that is delicious with a chilled red wine such as a Gamay or Cinsault from SOFT & JUICY! Rosé is also superb
Clam chowder	A rich, ripe Chardonnay from STONE FRUITS
Fish and chips	English sparkling wine!
Oily fish like sardines, herrings or mackerel	Dry sherry or a high-acidity white like a Chablis from ORCHARD FRUITS
Smoked fish such as salmon or haddock (think kedgeree)	Oaked whites are the order of the day here so a lightly oaked white Bordeaux made from Sémillon and Sauvignon Blanc (CITRUS FRUITS and GREEN FRUITS & GRASS blend) or a Chardonnay from STONE FRUITS
Seafood curries	An off-dry Pinot Gris, Riesling or Gewürztraminer from EXOTIC FRUITS & SPICE

Red Meat, Pork & Game

If serving red meat or game then a red wine of some description is absolutely the way to go. Not only do you want to match the weight of the wine with the weight of the dish but rich, fatty meats soften both the acidity and tannins found in red wines as they bind with the proteins in the meat. This means that now is the time to bust out those powerful reds with firm tannins as they will taste softer – have you ever noticed that your red wine can seem quite different once you have finished your meal and are enjoying the last glass on its own? As ever, attention needs to be paid both to how the meat is cooked and whether it is being served with any sort of sauce (our friend flavour balancing), both of which are likely to be influenced by the time of year.

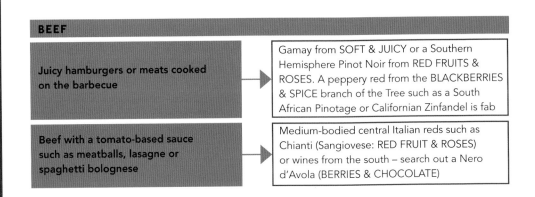

BEEF

Juicy hamburgers or meats cooked on the barbecue	Gamay from SOFT & JUICY or a Southern Hemisphere Pinot Noir from RED FRUITS & ROSES. A peppery red from the BLACKBERRIES & SPICE branch of the Tree such as a South African Pinotage or Californian Zinfandel is fab
Beef with a tomato-based sauce such as meatballs, lasagne or spaghetti bolognese	Medium-bodied central Italian reds such as Chianti (Sangiovese: RED FRUIT & ROSES) or wines from the south – search out a Nero d'Avola (BERRIES & CHOCOLATE)

Roast beef, stews, casseroles, steaks or pies	→	A robust red such as a full-bodied bottle from the CURRANTS & HERBS or BLACKBERRIES & SPICE branch would be a winning match
Beef chilli or a curry	→	A ripe red from the BERRIES & CHOCOLATE branch such as a Merlot or Nero d'Avola or BLACKBERRIES & SPICE such as a Shiraz

LAMB

Roast lamb, lamb shanks, shepherd's pie, lamb chops or rack of lamb	→	Sensational with Cabernet Sauvignon from the CURRANTS & HERBS branch; the minty notes act like mint sauce
Lamb in a spicy sauce such as a curry	→	A fruity, flavourful Southern Hemisphere such as a Malbec or Shiraz from BLACKBERRIES & SPICE. The key is to have a wine with very little tannin as they clash with the spice

PORK

Sticky ribs	→	Ribs with sticky sauces and marinades are delicious with ripe, fruit-forward, warm-climate reds like a full-bodied Shiraz (BLACKBERRIES & CHOCOLATE)
Roast pork, pork chops or gammon	→	Pork is quite versatile. For a white, enjoy Chenin Blanc (especially from South Africa) or a Chablis – both ORCHARD FRUITS – but also a juicy Pinot Noir from the RED FRUITS & ROSES branch
Sausages and charcuterie	→	A juicy red such as a Cinsault or Gamay from SOFT & JUICY or a lighter Pinot Noir or Grenache from RED FRUITS & ROSES

VENISON & GAME

Venison, pheasant, grouse and partridge	→	Elegant reds with acidity from the RED FRUITS & ROSES branch are ideal but for something with a bit more structure – if having a game pie for example – then try Barbera from the BERRIES & CHOCOLATE branch or a richer Tempranillo

Vegetables

The versatility of vegetables means that they can be matched with a wide range of different wines although generally whites work better, especially if they have any green or herbal notes such as tomato leaf or green pepper. To help narrow down your options to make a great match, think seasonally and think about the branches of the Wine Flavour Tree that best suit the season that your chosen vegetable is harvested in. Spring veggies are amazing with Sauvignon Blanc, whilst summer produce works really well with lighter whites. Autumn's starchier root vegetables require riper, more structured varieties but for mushrooms (including truffles), you'll want to consider reaching for a red berry-scented bottle. However, once they are in richer, more textured dishes like a risotto, then a white wine works just as well, cutting through the intensity to lift the dish and refresh the palate, ready for another bite.

Green vegetables such as asparagus, broccoli, kale or green peppers	A herbal Sauvignon Blanc from the GREEN FRUITS & GRASS branch is a superlative match
Light and delicate salads	Summery whites from the ORCHARD FRUITS branch like Pinot Grigio or Garganega (Soave) are great, or try a Sauvignon Blanc (GREEN FRUITS & GRASS)
Corn on the cob	A zesty white from the CITRUS FRUITS branch such as a dry Riesling or Sémillon
Tomatoes: either in a salad or as the base for a dish such as a pizza or pasta sauce	Sauvignon Blanc (GREEN FRUITS & GRASS) and tomatoes are a match made in heaven due to the tomato leaf flavours in some wines. For a red, try a Chianti from the RED FRUITS & ROSES branch of the Tree
Tuna Niçoise or a peach and prosciutto salad	A stunning match is a cool, crisp glass of summery rosé! For a white wine, try a Chablis (unoaked Chardonnay) from ORCHARD FRUITS
Starchy, autumnal root vegetables such as butternut squash and parsnips	Riper, more structured whites such as a Chardonnay or Viognier from the STONE FRUITS branch are needed here
Mushrooms or truffle-flavoured umami dishes	A Pinot Noir or northern Italian red such as a Barbera or Nebbiolo (all from the RED FRUITS & ROSES branch). If the mushrooms are in a creamier dish such as a risotto or stroganoff then a white would be a superior choice: Fiano or Chardonnay from STONE FRUITS
Sweeter root vegetables such as parsnips and beetroot	Open a delicately aromatic varietal such as an off-dry Riesling or Gewürztraminer from EXOTIC FRUITS & SPICE
Nut roast or a vegetarian Wellington	Veggie dishes with lots of flavour work well with rustic wintery reds such as southern French Grenache-based blends – think Châteauneuf-du-Pape or a Côtes du Rhône from the RED FRUITS & ROSES branch or a peppery Syrah from BLACKBERRIES & SPICE

Cheese & Dairy

The most surprising thing when it comes to cheese and dairy, and the mixed cheeseboard in particular, is that white wines actually work better overall, not reds! As is often the case, if you had to choose one wine to match the myriad of different flavours, it would be a Chardonnay, or even champagne, because the acidity cuts through rather than clashes with the fat of the cheese, which some tannic reds can. While lighter cheeses favour lighter whites, when you start to consider stronger types you need to consider more characterful wines, reaching for aromatic varieties for stinky cheeses and fortified and sweet wines for salty blues. Outside of the cheeseboard, the key thing to consider is the 'contrast or complement' question … you can either cut through a dairy-based dish with a fresher white or reach for one that is richer to marry well with the meal.

Lightly flavoured cheese such as mozzarella	A lightly flavoured cheese needs a lightly flavoured wine so reach for one from the ORCHARD FRUITS branch: a Pinot Grigio
Lighter-flavoured soft cheeses – goat's cheese or feta	Sauvignon Blanc from the GREEN FRUITS & GRASS branch is hard to beat with goat's cheese, especially a crisp Sancerre
Stronger-flavoured soft cheeses – Brie or Camembert	These riper cheeses work well with champagne, a Chenin Blanc from ORCHARD FRUITS or a juicy red from either the SOFT & JUICY or RED FRUITS & ROSES branch such as a Gamay or Pinot Noir
Harder cheese such as Comté	Champagne or a Crémant are spot on here
Parmesan	A versatile cheese that works with white, red and sparkling wines. A delicious choice is a soft red from BERRIES & CHOCOLATE like Barbera or a Garnacha from RED FRUITS & ROSES
Manchego	For this Spanish cheese, try a richer sherry such as an Oloroso
Aged Cheddar	Aged Cheddar is a good match with both white and red wine. For a white, try a riper Chardonnay from the STONE FRUITS branch and for red, something with some tannin like a Cabernet Sauvignon from CURRANTS & HERBS
Stinky, strong cheese such as Munster, Époisses and Stinking Bishop	A lightly aromatic Gewürztraminer from the EXOTIC FRUITS & SPICE branch is sensational
Blue, veiny cheese like Stilton or Roquefort	A classic match with sweet or fortified wines such as port
Other cheesy dishes outside of the cheeseboard: carbonara (Parmesan) or cauliflower cheese (Cheddar)	A white wine is the answer here and if you were going down the 'complement' route then a lightly oaked Chardonnay from STONE FRUITS would be a great match or a fresher white such as a Sémillon from CITRUS FRUITS or even a Soave from ORCHARD FRUITS

Puddings & Desserts

When it comes to sweet treats, the essential thing to remember is that the wine needs to be sweeter than the food, otherwise the sweetness of the pudding will make the wine seem acidic and dry. Therefore, the sweeter the dessert, the richer and sweeter the wine needs to be to cope with the dish. For lighter, summery, fruit-based desserts full of either citrus fruits, seasonal red berries – think cherries and strawberries – or even tropical fruits, fruity sweeties with fresh acidity are the order of the day. Also consider the primary flavour of your dessert and look for sweet wines that echo those flavours; an apple-based pud is superb with apple-flavoured stickies for example. Really rich and decadent desserts benefit from equally unctuous and even fortified wines. Turn to p. 254 for more information on these delicious styles so that you can enjoy them all the more.

Lighter, summery, fruit-based puddings such as lemon tarts, red fruit pavlovas or tropical fruit-laden meringues	A pretty, grape-scented Muscat, a sparkling Moscato d'Asti or a sweet Riesling – all found on the EXOTIC FRUITS & SPICE branch
Apple-based puds such as pies, tarte Tatin or a crumble	An apple-scented sweetie from the Loire like a Vouvray (make *sure* it is a sweet one) or a Coteaux du Layon are excellent choices, both made from Chenin: ORCHARD FRUITS
Afternoon tea and cakes	Off-dry sparkling rosés are fantastic with sandwiches, cakes and scones or a pink champagne. Asti is a cheaper choice
Crème caramel	A lightly honeyed and orange blossom-scented Sauternes made from a blend of Sémillon (CITRUS FRUITS), Sauvignon Blanc (GREEN FRUITS & GRASS) and Muscadelle
Banoffee pie	Richer sweeties such as a Hungarian Tokaji
Chocolate – milk or dark	Chocolate is notoriously hard to match but tawny and red ports and sweeter sherries work well, as do classic French Vin Doux Naturel wines such as Banyuls, Maury or Muscat de Beaumes-de-Venise (the latter found on EXOTIC FRUITS & SPICE)
Chocolate – white	Choose a sweet Riesling or a Moscato d'Asti – look to EXOTIC FRUITS & SPICE
Christmas pudding, Christmas cake and mince pies	My favourite match is Rutherglen fortified Muscat which bursts with notes of raisins and orange. Sweeter tawny ports, richer sherries and Tokaji are all good too
Ice cream	The supremely sweet Pedro Ximénez (PX) sherry is a decadent choice to pour over vanilla ice cream!

'Wine speak' can often feel like a whole new language. I hope the following guide will help you get to grips with this new vocabulary.

YOUR WINE
DICTIONARY

The Structure of Wine

Acidity: the part of the wine that makes your mouth create saliva and is responsible for refreshing the palate. The pH is linked to the colour as well as the stability of the wine. High acid wines tend to come from cooler climates, though winemakers from warm to hot climates such as Australia are allowed to acidify their wines through the addition of acids naturally found in wine – tartaric and malic

Alcohol: this contributes significantly to the structure of a wine and can be detected by the legs or tears on the glass: the greater or more visible they are, the higher the alcohol. If the alcohol is too high and out of balance then the wine can seem 'hot' on the finish, meaning there's a slight warmth at the back of the mouth

Aroma: what a wine smells like

Balance: arguably one of the most important words in wine tasting and the most important measure of quality. For a wine to be deemed good (or even great), the fundamental components have to be in balance – the fruit, acidity, alcohol and tannin (for red). If a wine fills your whole mouth and is harmonious, with nothing jarring, then the wine is well balanced

Body (mouthfeel): the weight and structure of the wine – light-bodied, medium-bodied or full-bodied. Is the wine delicate and ethereal or heavy, rich and ripe? A wine can also be thin, which means lacking in body

Fruit (flavour): the fruit profile or flavour of the wine is derived from the grape variety and the fermentation process, as esters (chemical compounds) are produced, which tend to impart notes like pear, apricot and peach to the wines. Some can be quite neutral or restrained when it comes to flavour – like the Orchard Fruits branch of the Tree – while others can be more aromatic and expressive: Exotic Fruits & Spice

Length (or finish): this is simply how long you can taste the wine in your mouth for after you have either spat it out or swallowed it. The longer the length or aftertaste, the better the quality of the wine; if it is short or fades quickly, that indicates that the wine isn't a great one

Quality: there are four things that can help you determine the quality of a wine and they form the acronym BLIC: balance, length, intensity and complexity. Balance and length are discussed above; intensity means the depth of fruit or how it perseveres in the mid-palate, and complexity refers to how many layers there are to the wine. Is it interesting, nuanced and intriguing or all upfront fruit that shouts blackcurrants but then fades away to nothing? Initially, quality is one of the trickier things to assess

Tannin: a 'polyphenol', predominantly found in the skins of the grapes, though also in the seeds, stalks and in oak – so you can get both fruit tannin and oak tannin in wine. Because tannin is found in the skins it is through the process of skin contact – where the juice of the grape is left in contact with the skins (predominantly a red and orange winemaking process) – that tannin gets leached out

Common Wine Faults

Acetic acid: this is created when acetic acid bacteria turns ethanol, or alcohol, into vinegar

Brettanomyces: a spoilage yeast that has two different strains: 4EG, which smells of calamine lotion and spice, and 4EP, which smells more like manure! The 'Brettier' the wine, the less appealing it is, as it tends to dry out the fruit and highlight the structure of a wine so that it can appear a bit charmless and tannic. I have never come across a white wine with this problem

Cork taint or TCA: this occurs when a wine is affected by something called TCA or 2,4,6-trichloroanisole, which is usually, though not always, transferred via the cork. The wine tends to smell mouldy, woody and cardboardy – quite different from the notes of spice, dill or vanilla you would expect to get from oak. This is the most prevalent and consequently the most significant wine fault

Fizzy: a wine can be intentionally slightly sparkling, with a prickle of spritz for freshness, but sometimes a wine can re-ferment in bottle and the by-product of carbon dioxide gives the wine an unwanted fizziness. There might be a haze, too

Oxidation: sherry, for example, goes through a deliberate oxidation to give the wine its distinctive taste, but if your wine smells in any way of sherry and is coupled with a slight orange hue, then the chances are it's oxidised, perhaps due to a fault in the closure or how it has been made or stored. Natural wines can display this fault due to a lack of sulphur in the winemaking process

Reduction: a tricky one to spot, to be honest. It's a slightly unpleasant savoury sort of smell, the result of the wine not being exposed to enough oxygen, and is more commonly found in screwcap bottles

Other Lingo

Aggressive: when the wine has too much acidity, alcohol or tannin with not enough fruit. If the wine is astringent, the term tends to refer to the profile of the tannins which are a bit dry and rough

Aromatic: this is usually applied to white wines and those varieties that are especially 'lifted' – i.e. they have a distinct aroma – such as Gewürztraminer, Muscat and Riesling, but can also include Viognier and Sauvignon Blanc – any variety, really, with an elevated aroma

Baked (also jammy): when the wine is from a hot region and made from overripe grapes that were literally left to bake in the sun, giving flavours of baked fruits – prunes and figs, for example

Big: as you might expect, a wine that is full of everything: flavour, alcohol, tannin and oak

Blanc de Blancs: traditional method sparkling wines made only from white grapes

Blanc de Noirs: traditional method sparkling wines made only from red grapes

Brooding: a deep, inky, red wine that is a bit tight, young and closed but will hopefully improve by opening up and softening

Buttery: a buttery flavour (and texture) predominantly comes from diacetyl, which is a by-product of malolactic fermentation – when tart malic acid is converted by bacteria into softer lactic acid

Chaptalisation: when sugar is added to a wine BEFORE fermentation to increase the alcohol of the wine rather than the sweetness

Chewy: when the tannins are quite grippy and firm

Clarification (also stabilisation): essentially cleaning the wine and making it stable

Clean: when a wine has no faults

Climat: a specific vineyard site in Burgundy, France

Closed (also dumb): when the wine gives very little away when smelling it – a particular problem of neutral grape varieties and wines served too cold

Cloying: when the acidity of the wine is too low

Complete: when the wine is in balance and harmonious

Complex: when a wine is multi-faceted, layered and interesting

Crisp: a positive term meaning attractive, fresh acidity

Declaration: when a port house/producer 'declares' a vintage, essentially saying that they deem their grapes to be of the highest quality and can thus make a vintage port

Delicate: the opposite to big; when a wine is light-bodied and subtle. Can be used both as a pejorative term and as a compliment depending on the context

Depth: similar to complexity and linked to quality – does the wine have good mid-palate weight? If there's good depth of fruit it means the fruit is persistent and the wine is likely to be well made

Developed: when a wine is developed – rather than developing – it isn't going to improve and it's time to drink it up. The stage after developed would be dried out

Dosage: the final adjustment for traditional method sparkling wines to determine the sweetness of the wine

Elegant: when the fruit is restrained, with balanced acidity and tannin; not a shouty wine

Ethereal: usually a term used for Pinot Noir to describe the delicate, elegant nature of the wine

Extracted: if a red wine is described as being 'extracted' (or even 'over-extracted'), it suggests that the winemakers have been a little heavy-handed with the extraction of colour, flavour and tannin during fermentation and the wine is a touch full-on

Flabby: lack of acid so the wine is a bit fat and lacks refinement; similar to cloying

Flat: this doesn't just meant a lack of bubbles for sparkling wine, it can also refer to a lack of freshness or acidity. If the fruit itself is flat it could be due to the wine being faulty which can 'scalp' the fruit – i.e. diminish its intensity – which can happen if the wine was corked or 'Bretty'

Flinty: wines with distinct minerality can be called flinty, such as Sancerre from the Loire Valley

Fresh: young and lively with good acidity

Fruity or fruit forward: as it sounds, when a wine has a distinctive taste of fruit

Green (also stalky): this doesn't just mean a green fruit profile, which is a good thing, but also unripe fruit. A wine described as 'green' could be young and stalky as the fruit flavours didn't ripen properly possibly due to a poor, cold or wet vintage

Hard: while firm tannins can be a good thing, hard is when the tannins are too firm

Hollow: when a wine doesn't have enough mid-palate weight so is not complete or harmonious

Hot: when the alcohol is too high

Horizontal tasting: when you taste the same vintage of different wines

Honeyed: a wine might be described as honeyed if it is a sweet wine, a Chablis or a Chenin Blanc. Notes of honey can also be found in some whites that are starting to tire

Juicy: used for wines that are really young, not terribly structured and full of fruit

Legs (also tears): indicate the alcoholic content of a wine (see Alcohol, p. 282)

Low Intervention: a 'hands-off' approach to winemaking

Luscious: if a wine is sweet and rich – a term used for pudding wines

MLF (malolactic fermentation): a bacterial conversion, when harsh malic acid (apples) is converted to softer lactic acid (milk), which gives a softer texture to the wines

Mousse: another name for the foam that forms on sparkling wine once poured

Must: crushed, unfermented grape juice, skins, seeds and stems

Nose: if you 'nose' a wine you are smelling it post swirling

Oaky: many white and red wines have some degree of oak influence, either through chips and staves (for cheaper wines) or through oak barrels. These can add notes of spice, vanilla, coconut and butterscotch, depending on the type of oak being used. Tightly grained French oak tends to impart subtle notes of spice, whereas larger grained American oak imparts more distinct flavours

Residual sugar: the amount of sweetness in the final bottled wine which can be added or left after the ferment has finished and can be found not only in sweet wines but also in commercial blends to increase the perception of fruit ripeness

Restrained: this term can be used if a wine is subtle and elegant, but it can also be a polite way of saying that a wine is a bit dull

Riddling: this loosens the dead yeast lees or sediment in traditional method sparkling wines so that it ends up in the bottle neck as a 'plug' and can be removed

Smooth (also soft): a good thing – a smooth red wine is drinkable and pleasing with no hard edges

Spicy: spice can come from the oak, especially French oak, with notes of cinnamon or nutmeg, or from the grape, particularly varieties such as Syrah/Shiraz, Gewürztraminer and Grüner Veltliner

Structured: when the wine is more about the acid and the tannin than the fruit – and so usually applies to red wines. This is when you might choose to decant or age a wine

Sur Lie: can be found on French wine labels and means 'ageing on the lees'

Unctuous: a grape like Viognier is unctuous – meaning textured and ripe with a slightly oily, silky texture that can feel quite rich and even a little fat. The term can also be applied to rich, sweet pudding wines

Vertical tasting: when you taste different vintages of the same wine

Vieilles Vignes: a French term that translates as old vines

Vintage: the particular year that the grapes in the wine were harvested. Wines can also be non-vintage – when they don't come from one specific or named year

WHITE WINE TASTING TEMPLATE

Fill in the gaps and circle the descriptors that best describe your wine.

Name of Wine	
Vintage	
Region and Country of Origin	
Grape variety/varieties	
Affordability (price)	
Retailer	

SEE

Water White	Yellow Green	Lemon Yellow	Gold	Amber

SMELL

Orchard	**Citrus**	**Green Fruits & Grass**	**Stone Fruits**	**Exotic Fruits & Spice**
apple	grapefruit	elderflower	apricot	ginger
honey	lemon	gooseberry	nectarine	lychee
nuts	lime	grass	peach	mango
pear	tangerine	herbs	yellow plum	pineapple

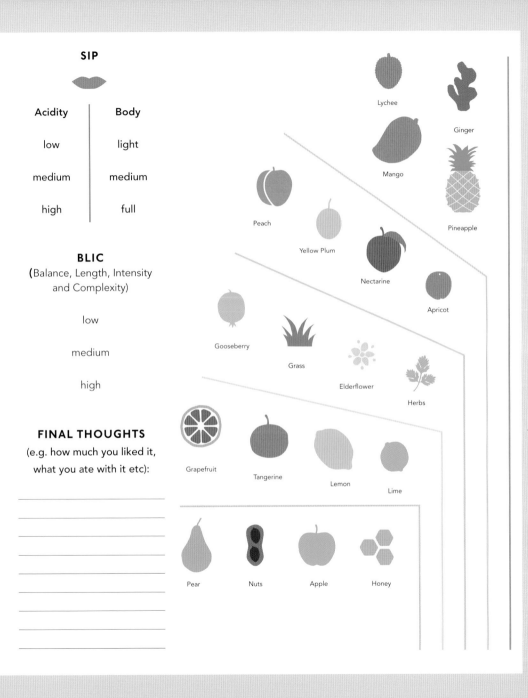

SIP

Acidity	Body
low	light
medium	medium
high	full

BLIC
(Balance, Length, Intensity and Complexity)

low

medium

high

FINAL THOUGHTS
(e.g. how much you liked it, what you ate with it etc):

Lychee

Ginger

Mango

Pineapple

Peach

Yellow Plum

Nectarine

Apricot

Gooseberry

Grass

Elderflower

Herbs

Grapefruit

Tangerine

Lemon

Lime

Pear

Nuts

Apple

Honey

RED WINE
TASTING TEMPLATE

Fill in the gaps and circle the descriptors that best describe your wine.

Name of Wine	
Vintage	
Region and Country of Origin	
Grape variety/varieties	
Affordability (price)	
Retailer	

SEE

Purple	Ruby	Garnet	Brick Red	Tawny

SMELL

Soft & Juicy	Red Fruits & Roses	Berries & Chocolate	Currants & Herbs	Blackberries & Spice
almond,	cranberry	blueberry	black cherry	bacon
banana	raspberry	chocolate	blackcurrant	blackberry
strawberry	red cherry	plum	blackcurrant leaf	black pepper
redcurrant	rose	tobacco leaf	violets	liquorice

SIP

Tannin	Body
low	light
medium	medium
high	full

BLIC
(Balance, Length, Intensity and Complexity)

low

medium

high

FINAL THOUGHTS
(e.g. how much you liked it, what you ate with it etc):

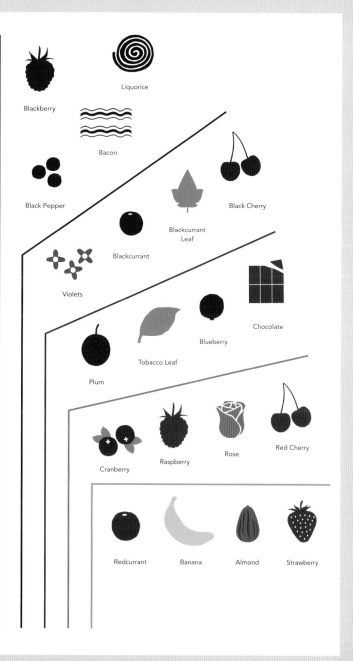

Blackberry

Liquorice

Bacon

Black Pepper

Blackcurrant Leaf

Black Cherry

Violets

Blackcurrant

Plum

Tobacco Leaf

Blueberry

Chocolate

Cranberry

Raspberry

Rose

Red Cherry

Redcurrant

Banana

Almond

Strawberry

INDEX

acetic acid, 284

acidity, 22, 41, 282

additives, 41–2

Adelaide Hills, Australia, 103, 182, 234

Alba, Italy, 158

Albariño, 29, 185–6

alcohol, 21, 60, 282, 288

Alsace, France, 144, 218, 220–21, 224, 233, 263, 265

Alto Adige, Italy, 144

Amarone, 265

Anjou-Saumur, France, 145

anthocyanins, 22

AOC classification (Appellation d'Origine Contrôlée), 70–71

Argentina, 113
  red wines, 113, 196, 229
  white wines, 145, 187, 222

aromas, 25, 26, 28, 52, 58, 282

Assyrtiko, 154

Asti, Italy, 128, 158, 265

Asti Spumante, 265

Aszú, 263

Auslese, 263

Australia, 132
  orange wines, 209, 211
  red wines, 111, 114, 156, 158, 161, 192, 196, 197, 227, 230, 234, 236, 238, 241
  sparkling wines, 132
  sweet wines, 261–2, 263
  white wines, 103–4, 108, 144, 149, 151, 182, 184, 185–6, 187, 218, 220, 223

Austria, 65
  classifications, 73
  sweet wines, 263, 264
  white wines, 149, 152

Bacchus, 29, 101, 105

Baden, 233

balance, 23, 282

Banyuls, 261

Barbaresco, Italy, 238

Barbera, 29, 196

Barolo, 63, 238

Barossa Valley, Australia, 151, 227

Beaujolais, France, 156

Beaujolais Nouveau, 156

Beaumes de Venise, 261

Beerenauslese, 263

biodynamic agriculture, 37, 38

Biodyvin labels, 37

Blanc de Blancs, 285

Blanc de Noirs, 129, 285

BLIC (balance, length, intensity and complexity), 23, 61, 283

body, 60, 282

Bonnezeaux, 263

Bordeaux, France, 102, 110, 115, 117, 151, 190, 228

Bordeaux mixture, 38

bottles
  opening, 84
  shapes, 74–5
  sizes, 86

Botrytis cinerea, 262–3

Botrytis wines, 262–3

Brazil, 231

Brettanomyces, 78–9, 284

Brunello di Montalcino 240

Bual, 261

'budbreak', 100

Bulgaria, 220,

Burgundy, France, 141, 180, 232–3, 286

Busby, James, 227

Cabernet Franc, 110, 117, 191, 264
Cabernet Sauvignon, 29, 109, 110–13, 190–91
Cahors, France, 228
calcium carbonate, 41
California, USA, 111, 184, 192, 197, 227, 230, 233, 238
Campania, Italy, 187
Canada, 36, 103, 156, 218, 220, 233, 264
Canterbury, New Zealand, 234
Cap Classique, 132
Carménère, 29, 109, 115
Carmignano, 240
Carneros, California, 233
Casablanca, Chile, 103
casein, 42, 49
cava, 131
Central Otago, New Zealand, 233
Chablis, 142–3
Champagne region, France, 76, 129
champagne, 63, 129–30, 233, 285
  Grand Cru, 131
  'grower champagne', 130
  non-vintage champagne, 130
  Premier Cru, 131
  production of, 130–31
  vintage champagne, 130
chaptalisation, 285

Chardonnay, 29, 129, 180–83
  unoaked Chardonnay, 29, 141–3
Chassagne-Montrachet, France, 180
Château Yquem, 263
Châteauneuf-du-Pape, 25, 227, 236
Chenin Blanc, 29, 145–6, 263
Chianti, 240–41
Chile
  red wines, 113, 115, 117, 192, 229, 234
  white wines, 103–4, 144, 184, 220, 222
China, 192
Cinsault, 29, 159
Clare Valley, Australia, 149, 218, 227
claret, 110
clarification, 41–2, 49, 286
Classic European wines, 62–5, 70
climat, 286
cloying, 286
Col Fondo, 128
colour of wines, 42–3
  orange, 45, 51
  red, 48–9, 55
  rosé, 46
  white, 43, 55
complexity, 23
Constantia, South Africa, 103
corks, 58–9, 84
  'corked' wine, 58–9, 78, 284

Cornas, France, 227
Cortese, 154
Corvina, 264
costs, 76–7
Côte Chalonnaise, Burgundy, 142, 181
Côte d'Or, Burgundy, 141, 232
Côte de Beaune, Burgundy, 141, 180, 232
Côte de Nuits, Burgundy, 141, 180, 232
Côte-Rôtie, 227
Côtes de Provence, 173
Côtes du Rhône, France, 236
Côtes du Rhône Villages, 236
Crémant, 131, 145
Croatia, 230
Crozes-Hermitage, France, 227

Dão region, Portugal, 114
decanting, 83
declaration, 286
Demeter labels, 37
depth, 286
Dolcetto, 29, 158
Dom Pérignon, 129
Domaine de la Romanée-Conti Romanée-Conti Grand Cru, 77
dosage, 286
Douro, Portugal, 114

Eden Valley, Australia, 149, 218

egg whites, 42, 49
Eiswein, 264
elegant wine, 286
Elgin, South Africa, 103
esters, 26, 27
European Union, 42, 70

Falanghina, 29, 153
fermentation vessels, 40
Fiano, 29, 187–8
Finger Lakes, USA, 218
fizziness, 284
flavour, 26–8
    see also Wine Flavour Tree
food and wine pairing,
    87–9
    autumn, 198–200
    cheese and dairy, 276–7
    fish and seafood, 270–71
    poultry, 268–9
    puddings and desserts,
    278–9
    red meat, pork and game,
    272–3
    seasons and, 87, 90
    spring, 118–20
    summer, 162–4
    vegetables, 274–5
    winter, 242–4
fortified wines, 254–62
    Madeira, 260–61
    port, 257–60
    Rutherglen Muscats,
    261–2
    sherry, 255–6, 257
    Vin Doux Naturel (VDN),
    261–2

France, 51, 62, 64
    classifications, 71
    red wines, 110–11, 115,
    117, 156, 159, 190–92,
    227, 228, 232, 236
    rosé wines, 172–3
    sparkling wines, 129–31
    sweet wines, 262–3, 264
    Vin Doux Naturel (VDN),
    261–2
    white wines, 102–3, 108,
    141–2, 145, 148–9, 151,
    154, 180–85, 188, 218,
    220, 223–4
Franciacorta, 132
Franken region, Germany,
    105, 219
Fréjus, 173
Friuli-Venezia Giulia, Italy,
    144
fruit (flavour), 282
Fumé Blanc, 103
Furmint, 263

Galicia, Spain, 185
Gamay, 29, 155, 156–7
Garganega, 29, 147
Garnacha (Grenache), 193
gelatine, 42, 49
Georgia, 65, 209, 211
Germany, 65
    classifications, 73
    red wines, 233
    sweet wines, 263, 264
    white wines, 105, 144, 149,
    218, 220, 224
Gevrey-Chambertin, 232

Gewürztraminer, 29, 220–21,
    263, 285
Gigondas, 236
Gisborne, New Zealand, 182
glassware, 82
Glera grapes, 128
glycerol, 22
Godello, 188
Gouais Blanc, 180
Graciano, 193
grapes, 20–21, 22
    grape skins, 22, 25
    grape varieties, 24–5, 63–4
    regional permitted
    varieties, 69–9
    rosé wines, 173
Grauburgunder, 144
Graves, Bordeaux, 110, 262
Greece, 65, 154, 223
Grenache, 29, 236–7
Grüner Veltliner, 29, 152

Hárslevelü, 263
Harvey, David, 209
Haut-Médoc, 110–11
Hawkes Bay, New Zealand,
    182
Hermitage, France, 227
Hungary, 65, 103, 220, 224,
    263
Hunter Valley, Australia, 151,
    227

Icewine see Eiswein
intensity, 23
International Wine
    Competition, 11

isinglass, 49
Italy
classifications, 72
orange wines, 209–10
red wines, 111, 116, 117,
158, 192, 196, 230, 233,
236, 238, 240
rosé wines, 173
sparkling wines, 132
sweet wines, 264–5
white wines, 103, 108, 144,
147, 153–4, 181, 187–8,
220, 224

Jerez, Spain, 255

Kamptal, Austria, 152
King Valley, Australia, 241
Kremstal, Austria, 152

La Londe, 173
La Rioja, Argentina, 222
Lambrusco, 128, 265
Languedoc-Roussillon,
France, 154, 184, 227,
236
late harvest wines, 265
lees see sediment
'legs', 21, 282, 288
length, 23, 283
Leyda Valley, Chile, 103
light strike, 79
Lodi, California, 230
Loire Valley, France, 102,
117, 145, 148, 228, 233,
263
Lombardy, Italy, 144

lutte raisonée, 37
Mâconnais, France, 142, 181
Madame Bollinger Medal,
10–11
Madeira, 260–61
Malbec, 29, 228–9
Malmsey, 261
malolactic fermentation
(MLF), 41, 285
Malta, 197
Malvasia, 264
Margaret River, Australia,
103, 151, 182
Marlborough, New Zealand,
103, 234
Marsanne, 188
Martinborough, New
Zealand, 234
Master of Wine (MW), 10
Maury, 261
Mazuelo, 193
McLaren Vale, Australia, 227,
241
Médoc, 110–11, 190
Melon de Bourgogne, 148
Mendoza, Argentina, 229
Merlot, 110, 190–92
Merret, Christopher, 129
methoxypyrazine, 109
Meursault, France, 180
Moldova, 220,
Montagny, France 181
Mornington Peninsula,
Australia, 234
Moscato d'Asti, 223, 265
Mosel, Germany, 149, 218
Mtsvane, 211

Muscadelle, 262
Muscadet, 148
Muscadet-Sèvre et Maine,
148
Muscat, 29, 223, 261–2, 263,
265, 285
Muscat Blanc à Petits Grains,
223
Muscat de Beaumes de
Venise, 223
Muscat de Frontignan, 265
Muscat of Alexandria, 223

Nahe, Germany, 105
Nantes, France, 148
natural wines, 50–51
Navarra, Spain, 236
Nebbiolo, 29, 63, 238–9
Negroamaro, 29, 109, 116
Nelson, New Zealand, 103,
234
Nero d'Avola, 29, 197
'New World' wines, 62
New Zealand, 38, 132, 263
orange wines, 209
red wines, 113, 192, 233–4
sparkling wines, 132
white wines, 103–4, 144,
152, 182, 184, 185, 218,
220, 224
nose, 288
Nuits-St-Georges, 232

oak, 102, 194, 288
barrels, 40, 41
flavours, 61
'Old World' wines, 62

Oporto, Portugal, 257
orange wines, 45, 51,
    208–11
    production of, 45, 51,
    209–10
Oregon, USA, 224, 233
organic wines, 36, 38
Other European wines,
    62–5, 70
oxidation, 78, 284

Palomino, 255
Perold, Abraham Izak,
    231
Petit Verdot, 110
Pfalz, Germany, 105
Picpoul de Pinet, 154
Piquepoul Blanc, 154
Piedmont region, Italy,
    196, 238, 265
Pierrefeu, 173
Pinot Grigio, 29, 144, 211,
    224
Pinot Gris, 144–5, 263
    off-dry Pinot Gris, 224
Pinot Meunier, 129
Pinot Noir, 29, 129, 180,
    232–4, 286
Pinotage, 29, 231–2
polymerisation, 23
Pomerol, 190
port, 257–60
    barrel-aged, 260
    bottle-aged, 258
    colheitas, 260
    Late Bottled Vintage
    (LBV), 258

ruby port, 258
Single-Quinta vintage, 258
tawny, 260
Portugal, 65, 154
    classifications, 72
    Madeira, 260–61
    port, 257–60
    red wines, 114
    white wines, 154, 185, 188
Pouilly-Fuisse, France, 181
Pouilly-Fumé, France, 102
Primitivo, 230
Prosecco, Italy, 128
prosecco, 128
Provence, France, 227, 236
Puglia, Italy, 116, 230
Puligny, France, 180

quality, 283
Quarts de Chaume, 263
qvevri, 209–10

Rasteau, 261
re-fermenting, 78
Recioto della Valpolicella,
    264–5
recipes
    Beetroot-Marinated Salmon
    with Harissa-Roasted
    Winter Veggies and Feta,
    246–7
    Butternut Squash Soup
    with Crisp Sage Leaves,
    202
    Cauliflower, Chickpea and
    Coconut Curry with Baby
    Spinach, 250

Chilli Con Carne with
    Shredded Beef, 206
Duck Breast with Red
    Cabbage and Potato
    Dauphinoise, 248–9
Grilled Tuna Steak Niçoise,
    170–71
Lamb Steaks with Spring
    Salsa Verde, 125
Lemon Chicken Salad with
    Bacon and Avocado, 167
Mexican Prawn Tortillas
    with Avocado Salsa and
    Grilled Sweetcorn, 168–9
Mini Venison Wellingtons
    with Parsnip Purée and
    Steamed Sprouts, 251–3
Pasta al Pomodoro, 166
Porcini Mushroom and
    Truffle Oil Risotto, 204–5
Posh Fish Pie, 203
Roast Chicken with Thyme
    Served with Spring
    Greens and Purple
    Sprouting Broccoli, 124
Tagliatelle with Asparagus
    and Lemon, 122
Trout Fillets with Crushed
    Peas, 123
red wines
    autumn reds, 189–97
    production of, 48–9, 55
    spring reds, 109–17
    summer reds, 155–61
    temperature, 81
    winter reds, 225–41
    see also colour of wines

reduction, 79, 284

regenerative viticulture, 37

residual sugar, 22, 288

Rest of the World wines, 62–5, 70, 132

Rheinhessen, Germany, 105

Rhône, France, 184, 227

Rhône Rangers, 184, 227, 236

Ribera Del Duero, Spain, 193

Ribolla Gialla, 211

riddling, 131, 289

Riesling, 149, 263, 264, 285

  dry Riesling, 129, 149–50

  off-dry Riesling, 29, 218–19

Rioja, 40, 193–4, 236

Riorat, Spain, 236

Rivesaltes, 261

Rkatsiteli, 211

Rolle, 108

Romania, 220, 233

rosé wines, 172–3

  production of, 46

  see also colour of wines

Rosso di Montalcino, 240

Roussanne, 188

Rueda, Spain, 107

Rully, France 181

Rutherglen, Australia, 223

Rutherglen Muscats, 261–2

saignée method, 46

Saint-Véran, France, 181

Sainte-Victoire, 173

Salento, Italy, 116

Salta, Argentina, 222

Sancerre, France, 63, 102, 233

Sangiovese, 29, 240–41

Santorini, Greece, 154

Sardinia, Italy, 108, 236

Sauternes, 262

Sauvignon Blanc, 29, 63, 101, 102–4, 110, 211, 262, 285

Savagnin Blanc, 220

Savennières, France, 145

seasons, 12–13, 14, 28–9, 87–9, 90, 94–5

sediment (lees), 39, 56, 83

Sekt, 128

Sélection des Grains Nobles (SGN), 263

Sémillon, 29, 151, 211, 263

Sercial, 261

serving wine, 81–5

sherry, 255–6, 257, 284

  amontillado, 256

  cream, 256

  fino, 255–6, 257

  manzanilla, 256, 257

  oloroso, 255–6

  pale cream, 256

  Palo Cortado, 256

  PX, 256

Shiraz, 29, 227–8

Sicily, Italy, 187, 197

Siena, Italy, 240

skin-to-pulp ratio, 25

Slovakia, 220

Slovenia, 209, 211, 220

Soave, 147

sommeliers, 10

Sonoma, California, 233

South Africa, 132

  orange wines, 209–10

  red wines, 113, 159, 192, 227, 231, 234

  sparkling wine, 132

  sweet wines, 263, 265

  white wines, 103–4, 144, 145, 151, 182, 184

sparkling wines, 57, 80, 85, 126

  ancestral method, 127

  carbonation, 127

  continuous method, 127

  English sparkling wine, 132

  opening, 84

  production of, 126–7

  sweet sparkling wines, 265

  sweetness levels, 133

  tank method, 127, 128

  traditional method, 127

  transfer method, 127

  transversage method, 127

Spätburgunder, Germany, 233

St-Émilion, 190

St-Joseph, France, 227

Steiner, Rudolf, 37

Stellenbosch, South Africa, 103

storing wine, 80, 84–5

straw wines, 264–5

sugar, 41

  residual sugar, 22, 288

sulphur, 36, 41, 49–50

sur lie wines, 39, 289

sustainable winemaking, 38

sweet wines, 262–5
  Botrytis wines, 262–3
  Eiswein, 264
  late harvest wines, 265
  sparkling, 265
  straw wines, 264–5
sweetness, 60
Switzerland, 156, 220, 233
Syrah, 29, 227–8

tannins, 22–3, 41, 60, 83, 283
Tarrango, 29, 161
tartrate crystals, 56
Tasmania, Australia, 149, 182, 234
temperature, 81
Tempranillo, 29, 193–5
terroir, 34–5
Tinta Barroca, 257
Tinta Cão, 257
Tinta Roriz (Tempranillo), 257
Tokaji, 263
Toro, Spain, 193
Torrontés, 29, 222
Torrontés Mendocino, 222
Torrontés Riojano, 222
Torrontés Sanjuanino, 222
Touraine, France, 145
Touriga Franca, 257
Touriga Nacional, 29, 109, 114, 257
Traminer, 220
Trebbiano, 264

Trockenbeerenauslese (TBA), 263
Turkey, 192
Tuscany, Italy, 264

United Kingdom
  red wines, 233
  rosé wines, 173
  sparkling wine, 132
  white wines, 105, 182
United States, 36, 132, 263
  red wines, 111, 114, 117, 156, 158, 192, 195, 196, 227, 230–31, 233, 236, 238
  rosé wines, 173
  sparkling wines, 132
  white wines, 103, 144, 145, 148, 182, 184, 185, 218, 220, 224
Uruguay, 185

Vacqueyras, 236
vegetarian and vegan winemaking, 49
Vendage Tardive, 265
Veneto region, Italy, 144, 147
Verdejo, 29, 101, 107
Verdelho, 261
Vermentino, 29, 101, 108
Vermentino di Gallura DOCG, Italy, 108
Victoria, Australia, 261
Vidal grape, 264
vieilles vignes, 289

Vin Doux Naturel (VDN), 261–2
Vin Santo, 264
vineyards, 34–8
  autumn and, 178
  climate, 34
  soil, 34, 35
  spring and, 100
  summer and, 138
  terroir, 34–5
  topography, 34
  winter and, 216
  yield, 35
Vinho Verde, 154
Vino Nobile di Montepulciano, 240
vintage, 71, 289
Viognier, 29, 184–5, 285, 289
viticulture 36
  biodynamic agriculture, 37, 38, 50
  Bordeaux mixture, 38
  lutte raisonée, 37
  organic, 36, 38, 50
  regenerative, 37
  sustainable winemaking, 38
Volnay, France, 232
Vougeot, 232
Vouvray, France, 145

Wachau, Austria, 152
Waiheke Island, New Zealand, 182
Wairarapa, New Zealand, 234

Walker Bay, South Africa, 234
Washington, USA, 236
white wines
  autumn whites, 179–88
  production of, 43, 55
  spring whites, 101–8
  summer whites, 139–40
  temperature, 81
  winter whites, 217–24
  see also colour of wines
wine, definition of, 20
wine faults, 78–9
Wine Flavour Tree, 14–16, 24, 28–33
wine intolerance, 50
wine labelling, 62–71
  classifications, 71–3
  laws, 70
  regions, 62–9

wine laws, 70
wine promotions, 77
wine tasting, 52–61
  aromas, 58–9
  colour, 54–6
  horizontal tasting, 287
  how to taste wine, 53–4
  swirling, 57
  taste, 59–61
  vertical tasting, 289
  wine faults, 78–9, 284
winemaking
  additives, 41–2
  carbonic maceration, 155, 156
  clarification, 41–2, 49
  fermentation vessels, 40
  intracellular fermentation, 156
  lees (sediment), 39

malolactic fermentation (MLF), 41, 285, 288
sparkling wines, 126–7
sur lie wines, 39, 148
yeasts, 39, 41
see also colour of wines

Yarra Valley, Australia, 234
yeasts, 39, 41
  yeast autolysis, 130

Zinfandel, 29, 230–31

ACKNOWLEDGEMENTS

I think it's fairly safe to say that I didn't have much of a clue about what writing a wine book entailed! I just knew that I wanted to write one and had what I thought was a strong idea that would translate well onto the page – so I 'simply' went ahead and did it. I now know that this is a fairly unusual approach and that it's customary to get yourself an agent, a publisher and a book deal first!

So the people I really want to thank first and foremost are those who turned this idea and rough manuscript from a dream into a reality and really 'got' what I was trying to say and do with this book from the very outset. I still remember being on a weekend away with a bunch of girlfriends when an email popped through from Hannah Schofield at LBA Literary Agency saying that her colleague Amanda Preston had given her my first draft and that she was excited by it. Reader, she signed me! Having someone who believes in you and what you are trying to do is obviously invaluable and Hannah did so right from the start. She also helped me to pull my synopsis and proposal together and astutely targeted the publishing houses she thought would be a good fit. Thank you so very much.

Again, I vividly remember exactly what I was doing (taking part in a twin study with my sister) when the email came through from Hannah saying that Square Peg – a boutique non-fiction imprint of Penguin Random House – wanted a meeting. As soon as I met the wonderful Marianne Tatepo I knew that she was absolutely going to be the right fit, and I wasn't wrong. She has stayed true to the real heart of the book but with a keen eye and a strong sense of what makes something readable, which has made it lighter, fresher and, without doubt, better. A million thanks, Marianne.

Her team are also awesome, from Graeme Hall's gentle guidance through the copy-edits to discovering that Emily Martin is a total ninja when it comes to turning a manuscript into a book and really understanding what looks good on the page. I salute you! Thank you too to Lucy Sykes-Thompson at Studio Polka for this fabulous cover (I love it) and the gorgeous artwork throughout.

I'd also like to thank a few people who helped me on my wine journey and got me to where I am today. To Chris Losh, who gave me the job of Tastings Co-ordinator at *Wine Magazine* (RIP) – I have no doubt that this role was a huge part of my Master of Wine success. It was also where I met the incomparable Charles Metcalfe, who taught me a thing or two about tasting, and Beverley Blanning MW, who became my mentor when I was studying to become a Master of Wine. You are all ace.

This book is already dedicated to my mum, but she deserves yet another mention. As I say in the 'background' section, it was at her suggestion that I even went into the trade and what a good suggestion it was; I've never regretted going into the wine industry, not for a single second. During lockdown I told her that I was going to write a book and my idea for it and I'm so glad she knew about this kernel of an idea. Tragically she died in 2021 before I'd even started and it breaks my heart that she didn't live to see this come to fruition. She'd have been so very, very proud. Grief put paid to starting this book for a while, but now it is finished and it is dedicated wholly to her for her selfless love, care and excellent mothering. I love you beyond words.

To my sisters Vicki and Katie: together we have had to navigate our way through this loss and I couldn't have done it without you. Eternally grateful to have you in my life. Also, huge love to Dad, Sue, Lottie, Sophie and Fred and the huge Jones and Caporn family clan. *In memoriam* to Roger too.

Finally, to the loves of my life – my husband Ed and my son Wilf. I honestly don't know what I did to deserve you both but you make my world go round. Thank you for everything.

ABOUT THE AUTHOR

I've been in the wine industry ever since graduating from university; so for my entire professional life. I started off working on the shop floor at Majestic as a trainee manager, knowing very little about wine, but started studying and gained a number of wine qualifications which culminated in 2011 with me becoming a Master of Wine (MW).

But, I remember all too well the time before I went to work in the trade, when I knew nothing about wine. Perhaps as a result of that, it turns out that my real passion is to educate people about wine. A little bit of knowledge goes a long way, and with wine being such a sociable, pleasurable experience, it's a really fun and useful subject to learn more about. In 2011 I also became a mother and decided to become a freelance consultant and set up as the Mistress of Wine, a pun on being both a female Master of Wine and an educator.

Photograph © Candice Lake

Work nowadays is a fantastic mix that includes consulting for one of the UK's largest discount retailers, being one of the six co-chairs at the International Wine Challenge and running corporate wine tastings. I also love writing about wine.